100
GREATS

SURREY
COUNTY CRICKET CLUB

The Bedser twins return to The Oval in 1946.

100 GREATS

SURREY
COUNTY CRICKET CLUB

COMPILED BY
JERRY LODGE

TEMPUS

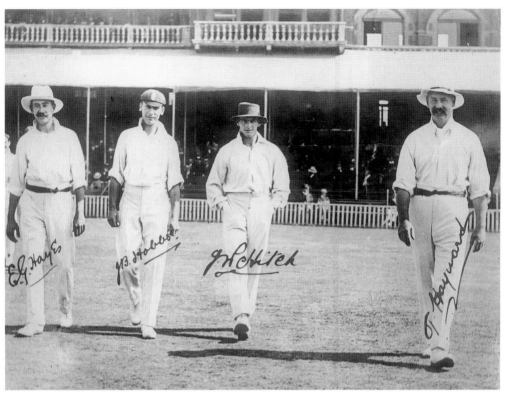

Four Surrey stalwarts take the field: Ernie Hayes, Jack Hobbs, Bill Hitch and Tom Hayward.

First published 2003

Tempus Publishing Limited
The Mill, Brimscombe Port,
Stroud, Gloucestershire, GL5 2QG

© Jerry Lodge, 2003

The right of Jerry Lodge to be identified as the Author
of this work has been asserted in accordance with the
Copyrights, Designs and Patents Act 1988.

British Library Cataloguing in Publication Data.
A catalogue record for this book is available from the British Library.

ISBN 0 7524 2742 3

Typesetting and origination by Tempus Publishing Limited
Printed in Great Britain by Midway Colour Print, Wiltshire

Dedication

By agreement with his brother, Adam, the current Surrey captain, this book is dedicated by the author to the memory of BENJAMIN CAINE HOLLIOAKE. When I was originally considering which players to include in the 100 Greats, Ben Hollioake was on the dividing line. With this dedication, I can increase the number to 101. His tragic death at the early age of 24 in March 2002 deprived Surrey of a dedicated all-rounder talent. His loss to the team is best expressed by the moving appreciation from his colleague, Ian Ward, in *The Cricketer*.

'Ben left an amazing mark on the lives of those who knew him. He lived a hugely full life and crammed so much in. Cricket was important to Ben, he cared more than he was at times given credit for, and the fires burned deep within him to succeed. He loved playing for England. But is was not the be all and end all for him. Ben wanted to live life and experience all of it'.

In seven seasons he played in 75 first-class matches, 66 being for Surrey. For the county he scored 2,267 runs at 23.61 including one century and took 190 wickets at 32.46 with a best bowling figure of five for 51 against Glamorgan at The Oval in 1999.

He played for England in two Test matches, both at The Oval against Australia in 1997 and Sri Lanka in 1998, probably too early in his career. He played 20 One-Day Internationals for England, his best score being 63 on debut against Australia in 1997 at Lord's.

His one-day career for Surrey was spread over 105 matches with a highest score of 98 in the Benson & Hedges Cup Final against Kent at Lord's in 1997. He scored 1,967 runs at 24.89 and took 121 wickets at 26.33.

The way that the Surrey team dedicated their 2002 season to Ben was so apparent as you watched them play. As Keith Medlycott said 'Their attitude was exemplary and I feel that the extra effort they were able to give has come from a deeper understanding of life itself'. Ben Hollioake had a cricketing talent that is sorely missed, and hopefully he will be remembered with affection through the Ben Hollioake Fund.

Acknowledgements

I am grateful for the assistance of Brian Cowley and Michael Pearce of the Surrey Statistics Group in checking the statistics for this book and Jeff Hancock, the Surrey librarian for proof-reading the script and his unfailing assistance in tracking down information and photographs. The majority of the photographs have been supplied from the Surrey Photo Library, but for current players much assistance has come from EMPICS.

Bibliography

Bailey, P., Thorn, P. and Wynne-Thomas, P.: *Who's Who of Cricketers*
Bartlett, Kit: Laurence Barnard Fishlock, *His Record, Innings by Innings*
Booth, Keith: His Own Enemy, *The Rise and Fall of Edward Pooley*
Cowley, Brian [Ed.]: *Surrey CCC First-Class Records 1845-2000*
Gover, Alfred: *The Long Run*
Green, Benny [Ed.]: *The Wisden Book of Cricketing Lives*
Hill, Alan: *The Bedsers – Twinning Triumphs*
Jones, Trevor: *268 – Alistair Brown*
Ledbetter, J.: *First-Class Cricket A Complete Record 1930 to First-Class Cricket A Complete Record 1939*
Lillywhite, Frederick: *Cricket Scores and Biographies*
Lillywhite, Frederick: *The English Cricketers' Trip to Canada and the United States 1859*
Lodge, Derek: *P B.H. May, His Record, Innings by Innings*
Lemmon, David: *The History of Surrey CCC*
Lodge, Jerry: *Ken Barrington, His Record, Innings by Innings*
Lodge, Jerry: *Sir Alec V. Bedser, His Record, Innings by Innings*
Lodge, Jerry: *Jack Hobbs, His Record, Innings by Innings*
Martin-Jenkins, Christopher: *World Cricketers – A Biographical Dictionary*
Overson, Chris: *Tony Lock, His Record, Innings by Innings*
Sawyer, David: *A Century of Surrey Stumpers*
Streeton, Richard: *P.G.H. Fender – A Biography*
Woodcock, John, *The Times One Hundred Greatest Cricketers*
Cricketer Magazine – various
Direct Hit – The magazine of Surrey cricket
Surrey CCC Yearbooks
Wisden Cricketers Almanacks

Introduction

From the formation of the club in 1845 until the end of the season 2002, the number of cricketers who have played first-class cricket for Surrey totals 632. In one-day cricket, which started in 1963, the county has used 128 players, the majority of whom have also played first-class cricket for Surrey.

The decision as to who are the best 100 cricketers to have represented Surrey has not been easy and despite applying very stringent criteria in the final analysis, it comes down to the personal opinion of the author.

The difficulties faced in deciding the final 100 cricketers is shown by those names who did not make the final list. They include J.E. Benjamin, M.C. Bird, M.P. Bowden, F. Burbridge, J. Caesar, Lord Dalmeny, H.M. Garland-Wells, D. Gibson, I.A. Greig, R. Harman, H.S. Harrison, R. Henderson, C.H. Hoare, B.C. Hollioake, T. Humphrey, G.G. Jones, G.J. Kersey, F.P. Miller, N. Miller, G.S. Mobey, W. Mortlock, W.E. Roller, L.E. Skinner, F. Stedman, G. Strachan, J. Street, R. Swetman and R.G.D. Willis. This is apart from players in the current team such as J.N. Batty, J.D. Ratcliffe and Nadeem Shahid not to mention the players who have recently joined the county, namely E.S.H. Giddins, J. Ormond and M.R. Ramprakash.

An analysis of the 100 cricketers selected shows that:
40 first played before the First World War, of which 11 went on to play after the war.
18 first played between 1919 and 1939, of which 13 went on to play after the Second World War.
42 first played after 1945 of which 10 are current players.

The twenty names shown in italics (in the list of the top 100 on page 8) are the top twenty Surrey greats. These were originally selected by Surrey Members and Supporters in 1995, but have been slightly altered by the author.

The statistics listed in the text show the number of matches played, which are classified as first-class and one-day matches [List A] as defined by the Association of Cricket Statisticians and Historians. For clarity figures relating to one-day matches are shown in italics.

Under the bowling section, where 5wI is shown for one-day matches this should be interpreted as 4wI.

The figures shown are those applicable at the end of the 2002 English season.

This book relates only to the playing staff, but an acknowledgement is appropriate to all the officials who have run the club over the years and the groundsmen who have prepared the excellent pitches at both The Oval and at Guildford.

100 Surrey Greats

R. *Abel*
M.J.C. Allom
G.G. Arnold
H.T. Barling
E. Barratt
K.F. *Barrington*
M.R. Barton
J. Beaumont
A.V. *Bedser*
E.A. Bedser
D.J. Bicknell
M.P. Bicknell
W. Brockwell
E.W.J. Brooks
A.D. Brown
F.R. Brown
A.R. Butcher
M.A. Butcher
W. Caffyn
T.H. Clark
S.T. Clarke
G.S. Clinton
B. Constable
J.N. Crawford
A. Ducat
J.H. *Edrich*
M.J. Edwards
P.G.H. *Fender*
L.B. *Fishlock*
D.G.W. Fletcher
A.R. *Gover*
R.J. Gregory
G. Griffith
E.G. Hayes

T.W. *Hayward*
J.W. Hitch
J.B. *Hobbs*
F.C. Holland
A. J. Hollioake
E.R.T. Holmes
G.P. Howarth
Intikhab Alam
R.D. Jackman
D. Jardine
D.L.A. Jephson
H. Jupp
K.J. Key
D.J. Knight
R.D.V. Knight
N.A. Knox
J.C. *Laker*
W.S. Lees
H.D.G. Leveson-Gower
P.J. Loader
G.A.R. *Lock*
W.H. *Lockwood*
T. Lockyer
G.A. Lohmann
A. Long
M.A. Lynch
A.J.W. McIntyre
A. Marshal
P.B.H. *May*
K.T. Medlycott
J.F. Parker
H.A. Peach
P.I. Pocock
E.W. Pooley

J.M. Read
W.W. Read
C.J. Richards
T. *Richardson*
G.J.R. Roope
T. Rushby
I.D.K. Salisbury
A. *Sandham*
Saqlain Mushtaq
J.W. Sharpe
T.F. Shepherd
T. Sherman
J. Shuter
W.C. Smith
J. Southerton
H.S. Squires
H.H. Stephenson
A.J. *Stewart*
M.J. *Stewart*
S.J. Storey
H. *Strudwick*
W.S. *Surridge*
D.A.D. Sydenham
G.P. *Thorpe*
A.J. Tudor
Waqar Younis
D.M. Ward
I.J. Ward
E.A. Watts
C.T.A. Wilkinson
H. Wood
Younis Ahmed

The twenty who appear here in italics, occupy two pages instead of the usual one.

Birth: Rotherhithe, Surrey 30/11/1857
Death: Stockwell, London 10/12/1936

Matches: 514

Batting career for Surrey:

I	NO	HS	Runs
813	59	357*	27609

Av	100s	1000s
36.61	64	8

Bowling career for Surrey:

Balls	Runs	Wkts	Av	Best	5wl
13785	5966	256	23.30	6-15	3

Catches: 492

Tests: 13, 1888-1902

A great favourite at The Oval, Bobby Abel, popularly known as 'The Guv'nor', began his career with Surrey in 1881, and played his last match for the county in 1904, his failing eyesight causing him to drop out of the XI earlier than otherwise he need have done. He was twenty-three years old when he first played for the county. Found in club cricket in Southwark Park, he took some time to accustom himself to new surroundings and his early efforts in first-class cricket gave no idea of the skill which he steadily attained. Very keen, he overcame the handicap of being short and while maturing his form with the bat, he attracted attention by smart fielding, especially at slip.

In his third season with Surrey he advanced rapidly as a batsman and in 1886, against the Australians at The Oval, he played a remarkable innings of 144. In 1888, one of the wettest seasons ever experienced, he came out first among the professional batsmen of the year, scoring in first-class matches 1,323 runs with an average of 31. Thenceforward, his successful career was interrupted only in 1893 when a serious infection of the eyes interfered with his play. If late in reaching his best, he was right at the top of the tree from 1895 to 1902, scoring over 2,000 runs in first-class matches in eight successive seasons. His highest aggregate of runs, 3,309, was obtained in

1901 and his average in these eight years of conspicuous ability ranged from 56 to 41. In 1903 his eyes troubled him again, though playing in glasses helped him to some extent. Next year his first-class career ended.

His highest innings was 357 not out against Somerset at The Oval in May 1899; it remains a Surrey record to this day. Besides this great score, Abel played eight innings of more than 200, and nine times in first-class matches he carried his bat through an innings.

Extraordinarily successful in Gentlemen and Players matches at The Oval, he scored 168* in 1884, 195 in 1899, 153* in 1900, and 247 in 1901. This 247 was the highest score ever obtained in a Gentleman and Players match until 1925, when Hobbs made 266 at Scarborough. For Players against Gentlemen at Lord's, his highest score was 98 in a memorable match in 1900.

Playing first for England against Australia in 1888, he took part in eight Test matches in this country, his best score being 94 at Lord's in 1896. In the winter of 1887/88, two English teams visited Australia. Abel went with G.F. Vernon's side and scored 320 runs in

average 48, more than twice the aggregate and average of any other member of the side.

A batsman of great resource and patience, he rarely if ever carried caution to an extreme and for a man of his small statue he was quite a punishing player. Once at The Oval he performed the rare feat of scoring 100 runs between 12 o'clock and lunchtime. He and Brockwell enjoyed many big partnerships together for the Surrey first wicket. Against Hampshire at The Oval in August 1879, they scored 379, a record for an opening stand at the time; 265 against Warwickshire at The Oval in September, 1898; 231 against Sussex at The Oval in May, 1897 and 270 (unbroken) against Kent at The Oval in 1900. Other great first-wicket stands in which he shared were 364 with D.L.A. Jephson against Derbyshire at The Oval in 1900; 246 with Tom Hayward against Sussex at Hastings in 1902, and 226 with W.G. Grace for South against the North at Scarborough in 1889. The biggest partnership of all in which he participated was one of 448 with Hayward for Surrey's fourth wicket against Yorkshire at The Oval in 1899, Abel scoring 193 and Hayward 273.

Abel drove hard and cut well, but his special strength came in his ability to get runs on the leg-side. Like many little men, he did not keep his bat perfectly straight, but accurate judgement of length of bowling and his quickness on his feet compensated for this defect. A very sure field, notably at slip, Abel also bowled slow off breaks skilfully but was not often wanted in the very powerful Surrey attack. Quiet and unassuming in manner, Abel was never spoiled by success. After one of his great days at The Oval, hundreds of his admirers would gather in front of the pavilion and chant 'Bob, Bob, Bob', again and again until the 'Guv'nor' bowed his acknowledgements. After his retirement he coached young players both at The Oval and at Dulwich College, whilst running a sports outfitter's shop in Harleyford Street, close to The Oval.

eleven-a-side matches, averaging 24. He was not chosen when the two parties joined forces on the occasion when Peel and Lohmann disposed of Australia for totals of 42 and 82. Abel went to Australia again in 1891/92 when W.G. Grace captained Lord Sheffield's side, averaging 38 in eleven-a-side games. At Sydney, in the second of three Test matches, he accomplished the remarkable performance of carrying his bat through the first innings for 132 but Australia won the contest when Alex Bannerman batted seven and a half hours for 91. Abel visited South Africa with Major Wharton's team in 1888/89 and scored 1,075,

Birth: Northwood, Middlesex 23/03/1906
Death: Tonbridge, Kent 08/04/1995

Matches: 100

Batting career for Surrey:

I	NO	HS	Runs
107	17	64	952
Av	100s	1000s	
10.57	0	0	

Bowling career for Surrey:

Balls	Runs	Wkts	Av
19500	7546	333	22.66
Best	5wI	10wM	
7-71	18	1	

Catches: 50

Tests: 5, 1929/30-1930/31

Maurice Allom achieved cricketing glory at Christchurch in January 1930, when he became the first man to take a hat-trick on Test debut and 4 wickets in 5 balls. He bowled Stewart Dempster with the second ball of his eighth over in Test cricket, then dismissed Tom Lowry, Ken James and Ted Badcock with the last three deliveries, reducing New Zealand to 21 for 7 in their first Test match. Allom only played four further Tests, all overseas. He was a highly effective amateur swing and seam bowler, as well as an active fielder for someone so tall. Being almost 6ft 6in, he had the height to make the ball come sharply off the pitch; he regularly dismissed good players and sometimes frightened them. Alf Gover recalled Arthur Carr, the Nottinghamshire captain, complaining to Percy Fender, leading Surrey, when he was flattened by an Allom bouncer: 'This is no way to play cricket, Percy.' Carr had Larwood and Voce in his side at the time!

Maurice Allom was in the Wellington XI for two years where he was coached by A.E. Relf, then went to Cambridge and gained his Blue in 1927 and 1928. Whilst at Cambridge, he achieved his best bowling performance of 9 for 55 against the Army in 1927. He was given a trial by Surrey in 1928 and then took eight wickets in his first three matches, but his appearances were gradually limited by the demands of his family business. In 1930, he was the highest wicket taker for Surrey with 67 wickets at 23.95. In 1931, he was injured with a leg strain and played only nine games. In 1932 and 1933 he was vice-captain of the club to Douglas Jardine. In 1932 he took 67 wickets, this time at 18.70.

His first-class record speaks of quality, playing 179 matches in which he took 605 wickets at 23.62, taking five wickets in an innings on 30 occasions and ten wickets in a match three times. His overseas tours were with Lord Tennyson's team to West Indies in 1928 and two MCC tours to Australia in 1928/29 and South Africa in 1930/31. His final first-class match was for Free Foresters in 1938.

He was a skilful saxophonist who played with Fred Elizalde's band in the 1920s, and wrote two well-received books, *The Book of Two Maurices* and *The Two Maurices Again*, with his friend and namesake Maurice Turnbull. Privately, he had a great sense of fun. This was less obvious when he found himself president of MCC in 1970, the year of the crisis over the South African tour, which was eventually called off after Government pressure. He followed this with eight less turbulent years as president of Surrey.

G.G. Arnold

RHB & RHFMB, 1963-1977

Birth: Earlsfield, Surrey 03/09/1944

Matches: 218 /52

Batting career for Surrey:

I	NO	HS	Runs
217	52	63	2302
92	35	24*	469
Av	100s	1000s	
13.95	-	-	
8.22			

Bowling career for Surrey:

Balls	Runs	Wkts	Av
36810	14857	745	19.94
7790	4001	227	17.62
Best	5wI	10wM	
8-41	32	2	
5-9	12		

Catches: 76 34

Tests: 34, 1967-1975
ODIs: 14, 1972-1975

Geoff Arnold's father was a good club cricketer and Geoff excelled at cricket when at school going on to represent ECSA against Public Schools at Old Trafford. Playing for Malden Wanderers for two seasons, he was introduced to Surrey Colts by Vic Ransom. He had a trial for Surrey in August 1961 and was offered a one-year contract.

He made his first-class debut in 1963, at the age of eighteen, against Derbyshire at The Oval, and in 1965, he was top of the Surrey averages when he took 77 wickets. He was capped in 1969, the year he took 109 wickets. He gave sterling service to Surrey over fourteen years with many excellent performances, invariably opening the bowling, his best match being against Gloucestershire at The Oval in 1967 when he took five wickets in the first innings and eight in the second. In the early days of the Sunday League, he took 5 for 11 toppling Glamorgan, also at The Oval.

Whilst many a fast bowler flags after the exertion of a few balls of an over, Arnold gave the impression of boundless stamina and endless willingness to go on attacking batsmen. That knees-up approach culminated in a side-on and a healthy circular sweep of the arm. The ball usually took anything but a direct course on to the bat, or the edge, or into the 'keeper's gloves.

Geoff first wore an England sweater – nobody ever saw him wear a cap – in 1967. Three wick-

ets against Pakistan at Trent Bridge was followed by 5 for 58 at The Oval together with an innings of 59 runs. His batting was interesting. The fast bowlers seem to rate it high enough to pepper him with bouncers from time to time; sometimes he hooked, and sometimes he just stood there, letting the ball whistle past, as if he was unaware that it had been released in his direction. In the early 1970s, he was one of the most effective bowlers in England and his Test place would have been more secure if he had been as deadly overseas as he was on the damper English wickets. However, two of his best performances were made overseas, 6 for 45 against India at Delhi in 1972/73 and 5 for 86 against Australia at Sydney on his last tour in 1974/75.

Geoff Arnold moved to Sussex and played for them from 1978 to 1982 with 77 first-class matches, before returning to Surrey as coach in 1984. He appeared in one Sunday League game for Surrey in an emergency in 1989. He lives for cricket and is still involved in coaching, acting as bowling coach to several first-class counties including Surrey.

H.T. Barling
RHB, 1927-1948

Birth: Kensington, London 01/09/1906
Death: Hastings, Sussex 02/01/1993

Matches: 389

Batting career for Surrey:

I	NO	HS	Runs
605	54	269	18995
Av	100s	1000s	
34.47	34	9	

Bowling career for Surrey:

Balls	Runs	Wkts	Av	Best	5wl
838	530	7	75.71	3-46	0

Catches: 171

Tom Barling was a stalwart Surrey batsman from 1927 to 1948. He made a highly successful start, having performed well in the Second XI, but lost form for four seasons until 1933, when he began a six-year sequence of scoring 1,000 runs every season. He was a naturally aggressive player but on forcing his way into the first team, he had played with a caution which was foreign to him, no doubt over-anxious to establish himself. Suddenly, he found it possible to throw off his inhibitions, and his batting began to flourish. The 1934 edition of *Wisden* said that for several years he had been instructed not to play his natural game of driving half volleys even when he had just come in. He almost left the club to join Middlesex. Returning to his own style, he scored 1,915 runs in the 1933 season, including 269 in just over five hours against Hampshire.

In 1934 he scored 1,184 runs with two centuries, being one of five players for Surrey to pass 1,000 runs in the season. Second in the county averages in 1935, he scored 1,538 runs, again with two centuries. The batting of the Surrey side continued to be strong in 1936, seventeen centuries being scored, four of which were by Tom Barling who scored 1,627 runs at 36.97. He scored over 1,000 runs in 1937 and the sequence continued in 1938 with five batsmen, including Barling, again scoring a thousand runs. 1939 was less productive. Throughout the 1930s, he scored prolifically in a style which E.M. Wellings said was as correct and pleasing as anyone in the game. Poised and quietly stylish he lacked extravagant mannerisms but was sufficiently highly thought of to be regarded as unlucky not to have won a Test cap. However, his stroke-play was far less assured against the fastest bowling and being on the plumpish side, he was not the greatest of fielders.

But in 1946, when he had turned forty, he was still good enough to pass 2,000 for the only time, including an unbeaten 233 against Nottinghamshire, sharing a partnership of 267 in under three and a half hours with Bob Gregory, on the August Bank Holiday weekend, when The Oval was packed. Alf Gover, who shared a benefit with him in 1946, said: 'Tom was a very fine strokemaker. He could hit the ball through the covers like anything. He was a very pleasant man too – full of fun.'

At the beginning of the 1948 season Tom Barling retired from first-class cricket and initially took up a position as assistant coach at The Oval, but later became coach at Harrow School, where he stayed until 1966.

E. Barratt

RHB & SLAB, 1876-1885

Birth: Stockton-on-Tees 21/04/1844
Death: Kennington, London 27/02/1891

Matches: 130

Batting career for Surrey:

I	NO	HS	Runs
210	48	67	1403
Av	100s	1000s	
8.66	-	-	

Bowling career for Surrey:

Balls	Runs	Wkts	Av
29349	12227	706	17.31
Best	5wI	10wM	
8-28	62	16	

Catches: 63

Edward Barrett created a sensation in 1872, when, as an unknown, he took 8 for 60 on his first-class debut playing for The North against The South in the second innings of the first important match that ever took place at Prince's ground, Chelsea. His slow bowling, left hand with a tremendous break, caused a great sensation, particularly when he disposed of six batsmen in four overs at a cost of only two runs. At Lord's, in the Whitsuntide match between the same sides, he took 7 for 18 in the second innings.

Having been raised in north-east England, he first became known as a cricketer when engaged as professional to the Longsight Club at Manchester in 1870. Two years later he was attached for one season to the groundstaff at Lord's and then he transferred his services to The Oval staff where in due course he qualified for Surrey by residence.

His connection with Surrey certainly formed the best and most prosperous part of his career. Playing first for the county in 1876, he remained a regular member of the team until the end of 1884. On the appearance of Lohmann and Beaumont, he gradually dropped out of county cricket. He took 100 wickets in a season three times, his best being 148, av. 17.25, in 1883. The best performance of his career was for Players v. Australians at The Oval in 1878 when he took all 10 wickets in an innings for 43. In the same season, he took 6 wickets for 34 runs against Nottinghamshire at Trent Bridge. In 1882, he was considered to be the recognised bowler of the team. He claimed 13 wickets for 73 runs against Oxford at The Oval and in the season delivered 998 overs for 1,439 runs and 93 wickets.

At his best, Barratt was certainly a very fine slow bowler, being able on certain wickets to get more work on the ball than almost any other cricketer of his generation. He was able to get an immense amount of break on from leg, and when at his best was very difficult to play, particularly for batsmen to whom his delivery was unknown. At times he was expensive, but when he did not try to do too much with the ball he was very dangerous. Although mainly a bowler, his batting came in great use to Surrey and he played more than one useful innings. In 1876 he made 40 in a low-scoring match against Sussex at Hove and in the same match he took 5 wickets for only 24 runs.

He also played for Durham (pre first-class, 1874/75). His final first-class match was for C.I. Thornton's XI in 1886. He was a first-class umpire from 1889 to 1890.

Birth: Reading 24/11/1930
Death: Bridgetown, Barbados 14/03/1981

Matches: 362 / 4

Batting career for Surrey:

I	NO	HS	Runs
564	99	207	19197
14	2	70*	399

Av	100s	1000s
41.28	43	10
33.25		

Bowling career for Surrey:

Balls	Runs	Wkts	Av	Best	5wI
9545	4729	133	35.55	5-46	4
108	132	4	33.00	3-41	

Catches: 382 5

Tests: 82, 1955-1968
ODIs: 0

Ken Barrington was born in Reading, the eldest son of a private soldier. He left school at the age of fourteen to take up an apprenticeship as a motor mechanic but a year later was offered a job as a groundboy at Reading CC which he gratefully accepted. In 1948, he joined the Surrey groundstaff and during the season had a game with Surrey Second XI against Norfolk.

After his National Service with the Wiltshire Regiment in Germany, he returned to Surrey where his progress was slow and he was fortunate to be retained on the staff. Under the fatherly eye of Andy Sandham, his batting steadily improved and his first match for Surrey was in 1953. He had a poor season despite scoring 81 against Worcestershire, but his form improved in 1954 averaging over 40 in the season and included sharing in a large stand of 198 with Jim Laker against Gloucestershire.

He made his Test debut in 1955 against South Africa and was dismissed for nought in his first innings. He was retained for the next match at Lord's but then dropped and did not play international cricket again until 1959. This was a time when he changed his approach to batting by eliminating every risky stroke from his repertoire and becoming the reliable and determined batsman that had so much success in his last ten years. In 1959, after scoring two centuries in one match against Warwickshire at Edgbaston, he won back his place in the England team against India. On the 1959/60 tour to West Indies, he scored his first Test century in a series won by England.

He became the most reliable of English batsman, the peak of his career being the 1962/63 tour to Australia with a Test batting average of 72.75 from five matches. By now he was the leading middle-order batsman for both Surrey and England and had become a highly efficient builder of long innings.

Apart from his smartly groomed appearance, his gear would be in perfect condition. His bats, normally a light 2lb 3oz size, were carefully chosen, clearly marked and lovingly tended. More than most, he was a nervous starter and he did not always do himself justice. At times, he had difficulty imposing himself on weaker bowling attacks and in 1965 he took over 7 hours to score 137 against a modest New Zealand side. This was the one flaw in his make-up and at times Surrey suffered from this apparent lack of aggression though he saved many a match through his stubborn batting. His leg-break

bowling had occasional moments of glory though he was never used on a regular basis. The Test match career of Barrington showed that his performances overseas were better than those in England. His career average against Australia was 63.97 from 23 matches and over 75 against India from 14 matches.

During his career, Barrington was involved in 142 century partnerships, twenty of these with John Edrich, sixteen with Micky Stewart and ten with Peter May. At The Oval in 1963, he hit 51 runs against Warwickshire in 13 scoring strokes, the fewest ever by a Surrey batsman in reaching 50. He made 1,000 runs in a season for Surrey 10 times. His highest partnership was 316* with Micky Stewart against Essex at The Oval in 1962. His career aggregate of 19,197 runs was the eighth highest for Surrey at the time of his retirement.

During his career, the one-day game was only in its infancy; Barrington playing in only 14 matches up to 1968 finishing on the winning side eight times. At the end of the 1968 English season, Barrington went to Melbourne to play cricket where he suffered a minor heart attack

and on doctor's advice retired from first-class cricket at the age of thirty-eight. With his wife Ann they ran a successful garage business in Bookham and Leatherhead. His son, Guy Kenneth, was born in November 1969, Ken and Ann having been married since 1954.

In 1975, he managed a tour to South Africa for Derrick Robins and was appointed as a Test selector. He was then the manager for the England tour to India, Sri Lanka and Australia in 1976/77 and the following year took the team to Pakistan and New Zealand. He was assistant manager on three tours, firstly to Doug Insole on the tour to Australia (1978/79), then Alec Bedser to Australia (1979/80) and Alan Smith to the West Indies in 1981. It was on this tour that Barrington suffered a fatal heart attack during a Test match in Barbados.

Surrey, through its Youth Trust, decided that a suitable way of commemorating Barrington would be to build a cricket centre with indoor nets and other sporting facilities. Her Majesty the Queen opened the centre in 1991 and it forms a lasting memorial to a great servant of the club.

Birth: Dereham, Norfolk 14/10/1914

Matches: 110

Batting career for Surrey:

I	NO	HS	Runs
183	13	132	3975
Av	100s	1000s	
23.38	5	2	

Catches: 79

In 1948, Michael Barton showed initiative as captain on the many occasions he deputised for E.R.T. Holmes and scored nearly 1,000 runs in the Championship, including two centuries. He was appointed captain in 1949, but his batting declined with only one century in the season.

Barton inherited a side that was changing in character. Of the pre-war stalwarts, only Fishlock, Squires, Parker and Watts were left. Watts played but five games in 1949 before retiring, and the season was to be the last for Stan Squires.

Michael Barton was, indeed is, a quiet, gentle man. His natural charm and courteousness won him many friends; his willingness to seek and listen to advice from senior professionals won him many more. Barton's achievement was remarkable when one considers that his first-class experience before 1948 had been restricted to two seasons with Oxford more than ten years earlier, yet he settled into the captaincy and carried out the job with ease, dignity and considerable success. 1950 saw Surrey sharing the County Championship with Lancashire, although Michael Barton rarely reached his best form. In 1951, Surrey found themselves without a reliable opening pair and after trying various people, Barton himself shared the duty with Eric Bedser. For the third time, Michael Barton scored 1,000 runs in the season in a year when Surrey finished sixth in the Championship. He decided the time had come to step down as captain, but had left Surrey a tidier and more effi-

cient side than he found them. Barton played only the occasional game for the club in 1953 and 1954.

As a youngster, he made a name for himself as a strong stylish batsman first at Winchester and then at Oxford. In 1932 and 1933 he scored 136 and 103 for Winchester against Eton and was in the Oxford XI in 1936 and 1937. He than went to Cornell University in the USA where there was no opportunity to play cricket. During the Second World War he was a captain in the Royal Artillery.

In his first appearance in first-class cricket he scored 164 for the Free Foresters at Oxford and he played for Norfolk from 1933 to 1947. A sound middle-order right-hand batsman, in his first four matches for Surrey in 1948 he scored 124 against MCC at Lord's, 132 v. Nottinghamshire at Trent Bridge and 103 v. Leicestershire at Leicester. He hit 1,000 runs in a season three times, his best year being 1948 when he accumulated 1,187 runs at 22.82. He was also a good slip fielder.

He was attached to a business firm in the City and was president of Surrey in 1983. A past president of the club, he is seen at The Oval on a regular basis.

Birth: Armitage Bridge, Yorkshire 16/09/1854
Death: Lambeth, London 01/05/1920

Matches: 91

Batting career for Surrey:

I	NO	HS	Runs
120	38	60	741
Av	100s	1000s	
9.03	-	-	

Bowling career for Surrey:

Balls	Runs	Wkts	Av
17982	6222	404	15.40
Best	5wI	10wM	
8-40	28	7	

Catches: 29

John Beaumont was born in Armitage Bridge, near Huddersfield. He appeared in his young days for Yorkshire but failed to make a name for himself in his native county, playing only 4 games during 1877 and 1878. From 1878 to 1882 he played for the Holbeck Club of Leeds. He was a carpenter and joiner by trade. An application for a place on the groundstaff at The Oval in 1883 was successful.

He must have been a promising bowler, as when playing for a local team against the Australians, he greatly impressed Blackman. He was practically unknown when, having qualified by residence, he made his debut for Surrey in 1885. He met with immediate success, causing quite a sensation in his first match, when he and George Lohmann dismissed Middlesex on a slow pitch for a total of 25, Beaumont taking 6 wickets for 11 runs. In the match he bowled 53 overs for 48 runs and 12 wickets, Middlesex being dismissed for 77 in their second innings. This performance made his place in the first team secure for the rest of the season and he fairly divided honours with Lohmann, taking 119 wickets in all matches at 15.52. Beaumont kept up his form for the next four seasons and though com-

pletely overshadowed by Lohmann in 1887 he had some share in winning back for Surrey, after an interval of 23 years, the first place among the counties.

In the winter of 1887/88, he went to Australia with Vernon's team. In 1888, he took 8 wickets for 40 runs against Yorkshire at The Oval and, in 1889, his next best career bowling performance was 8 for 89 against Derbyshire at Derby. For Surrey, again against Derbyshire, this time at The Oval, he added 118 for the last wicket, scoring 66 with Sharpe on 56*. However, he lost his bowling form in 1890 and 1891, playing in only one match.

At his best, Beaumont was a first-rate bowler, very accurate and apt even on the best wickets to get up to a nasty height. Standing 5ft 10½in tall and weighing 14st, he was quite individual in style, walking up to the crease to deliver the ball. His action was high, and, without being exceptionally fast, he could keep up a fine pace for any reasonable length of time. His very high delivery assisted him in making the ball break from the off with great straightness. A big, powerful man, Beaumont remained to the end of his life a Yorkshireman through and through.

Sir A.V. Bedser OBE CBE
RHB & RFMB, 1939-1960

Birth: Reading, Berkshire 04/07/1918

Matches: 370

Batting career for Surrey:

I	NO	HS	Runs
429	148	126	4108
Av	100s	1000s	
14.61	1	-	

Bowling career for Surrey:

Balls	Runs	Wkts	Av
76701	27918	1459	19.13
Best	5wI	10wM	
8-18	72	11	

Catches: 226

Tests: 51, 1946-1955

Alec Bedser was born in Reading, ten minutes after his identical twin brother, Eric. Their father was a bricklayer, and later in their lives, in 1953, helped his sons build their own house. They grew up in Woking and showed an interest in sport from an early age, playing cricket for a local club. At the age of fourteen, they started work as solicitor's clerks in Lincoln's Inn Fields, London.

When they were seventeen, Allan Peach, the Surrey coach at the time, opened a cricket school in Woking. The Bedsers were both medium-fast bowlers with identical run-ups and to give them a chance in pursuing a career in cricket, they decided, on the toss of a coin, that one should change his bowling style. Eric lost the toss and, with the help of Allan Peach, changed to an off-break bowler.

They joined the Surrey staff in April 1938. During two seasons, Alec played 24 matches for the Second XI, for whom he scored 229 runs and took 101 wickets at an average of 16.81. With Eric, he made his first-class debut against Oxford University in 1939, but they had to wait until 1946 before playing County Championship matches.

During the Second World War, the Bedser twins served in the Royal Air Force, spending most of their time abroad. However, before going overseas, Alec represented the RAF against the London Fire Brigade at Lord's, taking 4 for 44, and impressing, among others, Sir Pelham Warner.

They returned to The Oval in time for the 1946 season, by which time they were twenty-seven years old. Alec was awarded his Surrey cap on 12 June, and was picked to play in his first Test match against India after having played only 12 first-class matches. His dream start involved taking 11 wickets in the match, followed by a further 11 wickets in the next Test match.

The Bedser brothers were, and are, Surrey players and supporters through and through. In fifteen full seasons, Alec Bedser bowled 12,775.3 overs for his county – an average of 850 overs per season and 34 overs per match. He took 100 wickets in an English season eleven times, and in those years took 100 wickets for Surrey five times as well as more than 90 in four seasons. In 1953, Alec took 162 wickets in the season at an average of 16.67. In 1957, Peter May was appointed captain of Surrey and asked that Alec Bedser be made his vice-captain. In the rest of his career,

Alec Bedser captained Surrey in 74 matches of which 29 were won, 29 drawn and 16 lost. His best bowling performances were 8 for 18 against Nottinghamshire at The Oval in August 1952 and 8 for 18 against Warwick-shire, again at The Oval in May 1953, when Surrey won the match in one day. Alec Bedser continued playing for Surrey until the end of the 1960 season, taking five wickets in an innings in his last match, appropriately played at The Oval. Bedser played in 370 first-class matches for Surrey and there were only 30 matches in which he failed to take a wicket, analysed as follows: 6 matches outside the Championship, 24 Championship matches, of which 13 were during his last three seasons (1958/1960), when he was often captain.

From 1946 until the arrival of Tyson and Statham, he was England's prime pace bowler. During these years, he was both wicket-taker and stock bowler. In 51 Tests, Bedser bowled 15,918 balls; in 16 more Tests, Fred Trueman bowled 15,718 balls.

His greatest season was undoubtedly 1953 against the Australians, when he took 39 wickets in the series the year England regained the Ashes. Bedser was to play in only 4 Test matches after that season. He was a Test match selector from 1962 to 1985, and chairman of the selectors between 1969 and 1981.

From the proceeds of his benefit in the mid-1950s, later supplemented by Eric's benefit, the brothers established a typewriter and office equipment business in a small shop in Woking. In 1962, they went into partnership with the stationer Ronald Straker, and were subsequently taken over by Ryman and then Montague Burton.

Bedser was very proud to be elected president of Surrey CCC in 1987. His national honours include the OBE, awarded in 1964, the CBE in 1982, and a knighthood in 1997.

Birth: Reading, Berkshire 04/07/1918

Matches: 443

Batting career for Surrey:

I	NO	HS	Runs
669	78	163	14148
Av	100s	1000s	
23.93	9	6	

Bowling career for Surrey:

Balls	Runs	Wkts	Av
51255	19831	797	24.88
Best	5wI	10wM	
7-33	24	4	

Catches: 227

Eric Bedser is the elder of the Bedser twins by ten minutes and details of his early life are described in the section on his brother. He was not to reach the dizzy heights achieved by Alec, who often thought it unfair that the fruits of his and Eric's endeavours should have fallen to him alone. It might have been supposed that Alec's superiority as a cricketer would lead to friction, even an estrangement between the brothers. The most remarkable feature of their relationship is that each of them took the utmost pleasure in their respective achievements. Criticism was not withheld in their many post-match cricket conversations.

A more vexed point at issue was the situation in which Eric was placed in the Surrey ranks. As events were to prove, being an off-spinner he was set in opposition to Jim Laker. It has often been felt that had he not been in the same team as Laker, his reputation as a bowler would have been much higher. Ironically, the only time he was invited to an England trial match was at Bradford, where Laker took 8 wickets for 2 runs, with one run allegedly being given to Eric to get him off the mark. Eric Bedser generally bowled better when Laker was not in the Surrey team, having the first use of responsive wickets, but when Laker was on county duty, often he would not get a bowl.

Eric Bedser did overcome his disappointment in not advancing to international level by becoming a vital component in Surrey's suc-

cesses in the 1950's. He was deprived of the double in 1956 by the weather, scoring 804 runs and taking 92 wickets, but receiving praise from the captain, Stuart Surridge, who said: 'Without Eric in the side, Surrey might not have retained the title'. When Surridge took over the captaincy, one of his first decisions was to promote Eric to open the innings with David Fletcher. He was rewarded with sterling performances, and the new combination became one of the most reliable pairings in the country. During his career, he took part in 35 century partnerships, 31 of them for Surrey and 9 of them with Fletcher, including two double-century partnerships. In the six seasons when Eric scored over 1,000 runs he also took over 50 wickets in four of them. Seven wickets in an innings was achieved on four occasions, and ten wickets in a match four times.

Overall, his Surrey career figures compare well with Percy Fender, Eric scoring 14,148 runs and taking 797 wickets, whereas Fender scored 14,117 runs and took 1,586 wickets. Eric has given service to Surrey County Cricket Club throughout his adult life, receiving his county cap in 1947, being granted a benefit in 1958 and becoming president of the club in 1990.

D.J. Bicknell

RHB & LMB, 1987-1999

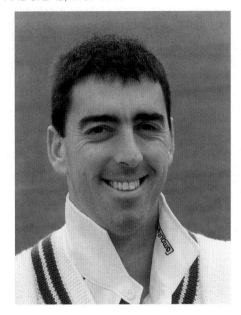

Birth: Guildford, Surrey 24/06/1967

Matches: 195 / 56

Batting career for Surrey:

I	NO	HS	Runs
343	33	235*	12464
152	21	135*	5080
Av	100s	1000s	
40.20	31	6	
38.77	7		

Bowling career for Surrey:

Balls	Runs	Wkts	Av	Best	5wl
1232	789	23	34.30	3-7	-
36	39	2	19.50	1-11	-

Catches: 73 37

In 1999, the 6ft 4in tall left-hander underwent six hours of surgery when a piece of hip bone was removed and used to fuse the lower vertebrae, where he had suffered a double stress fracture. Long fights and lonely vigils have been a trademark of Darren Bicknell. The friendly family man, once he became clad in the opening batsman's extensive armour, revealed a stubbornness and single-minded ability that drove opposition bowlers and fielders to distraction. It may not always have been pretty, though a vintage Bicknell innings had no shortage of flowing drives and elegant glides through the legside. But offer any cricketer the chance of a long knock every day, and you will find Bicknell near the front of the queue.

Nottinghamshire twice found themselves on the wrong end of Darren Bicknell's patience. When he hit 235* in 1994 at Trent Bridge, he batted for 10 hours 38 minutes, at that time the longest innings in first-class cricket. A year later, another 228* came against them in just 46 minutes fewer, this time at Woodbridge Road. In 1990, he shared in a stand of 413 with David Ward against Kent at Canterbury.

Although older than his brother, Martin, by 18 months, Darren was taken on the staff a year later, in the 1987 season. His ability to stick it out against hostile attacks won him that prized

contract at The Oval. His maiden century was against a Hampshire attack led by Malcolm Marshall on a pacey pitch at The Oval. Although suffering the familiar second season problems, he soon became established at the top of the order in a Surrey side which was being rebuilt under Ian Greig.

Along with Martin and Graham Thorpe, he was selected for the England A tour to Zimbabwe in 1989/90, followed the next two winters by trips to Sri Lanka and West Indies. Despite a century on a raging turner against Muralitharan, Bicknell never quite did enough to catch the selectors' eyes for the full side. Twice he just missed reaching his usual 1,000 and, in 1997, he spent half the season in the second team. As ever though, he fought back with two fine centuries to re-establish a place and seemed to have won his hardest battle. However, a back problem, which had increasingly troubled him over the previous two years, suddenly deteriorated while on a golf trip at the end of the 1998 season.

Unable to keep his place in the first team, Bicknell left the county for the 2000 season to join Nottinghamshire, where he shared a county record-breaking stand of 406 with Guy Welton against Warwickshire. The following year found him leading the county in most matches in the absence of injured captain Jason Gallian.

Birth: Guildford, Surrey 14/01/1969

Matches: 242 296

Batting career for Surrey:

I	NO	HS	Runs
292	73	110*	5218
151	64	66*	1335
Av	100s	1000s	
23.82	1	-	
15.34	-	-	

Bowling career for Surrey:

Balls	Runs	Wkts	Av
46161	21726	907	23.95
14266	9397	382	24.59
Best	5wI	10wM	
9-45	37	4	
7-30	14		

Catches: 86 69

Tests: 2, 1993
ODIs: 7, 1990/91

Martin Bicknell, at 6ft 4in, is one of the finest English bowlers of his generation, certainly the best not to have had a decent go at Test cricket, and Surrey has lapped up that selectorial oversight.

In 2000, Bicknell's finest performance came at Guildford, during Surrey's golden midsummer run. On a beautiful pitch, after his batsmen had conceded a lead, he annihilated Leicestershire with bowling that was hostile, quick and accurate. His 7 for 72 in the first innings, which he considers his best bowling of all, became 16 for 119 by the end of the match.

Bicknell is both a stalwart and a stylist, a classic English new-ball bowler: all shortish run, high arms and high knees, and a natural outswinger with the knack of cutting the ball back into the right-hander. Like Alec Bedser in the 1950s, he is the rhythmic heart of Surrey.

He was born in Guildford and was just what his older brother Darren had been waiting for. Bicknell went to play for local club Normandy when he was ten, opened the batting and bowling at school, and started playing Surrey age-group cricket. School was not his strongest suit,

and he left at sixteen, climbing straight into his whites. That summer he had an excellent season for Guildford and was rewarded with a Surrey contract. He made his debut in 1986 against Derbyshire at The Oval. *Wisden* tells of the seventeen year old who 'swept Derbyshire aside on the final morning by taking 3 for 4 in 11 deliveries'.

There followed two overseas tours with England Young Cricketers and one with England A (along with Darren) to Zimbabwe in 1989/90. He was then picked for England's 1990/91 tour of Australia and New Zealand. He did not play a Test, just seven one-day internationals, but he adored it. He loved being part of the set-up, the attention and the pressure, despite being battered, physically and emotionally. All of this made his subsequently brief Test career in the demoralising summer of 1993 – two Tests, 87 overs, four wickets, two ducks and a dodgy knee – so much harder to take.

However, playing for Surrey brought its own fulfilment. Bicknell had warm respect for his captain, Adam Hollioake. From 1998 to 2001, he scored 2,113 runs with the bat at an average of 32.50, including his first century and 12 fifties and took 268 wickets at 19.68.

As well as playing golf, he has set up his own business selling clubs and setting up tournaments.

Birth: Kingston-on-Thames, Surrey 21/01/1865
Death: Richmond, Surrey 30/06/1935

Matches: 314

Batting career for Surrey:

I	NO	HS	Runs
472	45	225	11830
Av	100s	1000s	
27.70	20	6	

Bowling career for Surrey:

Balls	Runs	Wkts	Av
25587	12273	500	24.54
Best	5wI	10wM	
8-22	22	0	

Catches: 219
Stumpings: 1

Tests: 7, 1893-1899

William Brockwell was a stylish and often brilliant batsman, strong in back play and a free hitter in front of the wicket. Combining a finished style with sound defence and brilliant hitting, he was an attractive batsman to watch. Brockwell also was a useful fast-medium-paced bowler and a smart fielder, notably at second slip where he succeeded George Lohmann, one of the surest catches ever seen in that position. Bright and genial in manner, he was a thoroughly popular cricketer.

First playing for the county in 1886, Brockwell, who was not a tall man (5ft 9in), matured slowly, but it was difficult for him to find a place in the very powerful Surrey XI of that period. However, from 1891 to 1902, he was a regular member of the side and he played his last game in 1903 when the team was declining rapidly in all-round strength. During Brockwell's career at The Oval, Surrey carried off the Championship eight times and once tied for first place with Lancashire and Nottinghamshire.

He exceeded 1,000 runs in a season six times, his highest aggregate being 1,686, average 38.23. In 1894, he headed the national first-class averages, in a season that was a difficult one for batsmen. He was also leading scorer for Surrey with 1,091 runs at an average of 35, remarkable figures in a summer of unsettled weather. His highest score was 225 for Surrey against Hampshire at The Oval in 1897.

Among his notable partnerships for Surrey were three with Bobby Abel for the first wicket – 379 against Hampshire in 1897, 270 unfinished *v.* Kent in 1900 and 231 against Sussex in 1897, all at The Oval. In 1895, Henry Wood and Brockwell added 146 for the ninth wicket against Somerset in 1895, again at The Oval.

He appeared for the Players against the Gentlemen between 1894 and 1902. His single visit to Australia in 1894/95 was not particularly successful. He had previously been to South Africa with W.W. Read's team, but this tour was not classified as first-class, although he was regarded as an excellent coach. In 1899, he took 105 wickets, at 25.26, his best season with the ball, and he completed the double that year. This included one spell of three wickets in five balls against Gloucestershire at Cheltenham. Previously, he had excellent performances of 9 for 20 against Essex at The Oval in 1893 and 8 for 22 against Warwickshire, also at The Oval in 1895. In 1900 he took 5 for 13, again against Essex at The Oval, and he achieved a hat-trick against Yorkshire at Sheffield. During his last three years at Surrey (1901-1903), he played some games for London County.

He fell on hard times after leaving first-class cricket and died in abject poverty.

E.W.J. Brooks

RHB & WK, 1925-1939

Birth: Camberwell, London 06/07/1898
Death: Rustington, Sussex 10/02/1960

Matches: 354

Batting career for Surrey:

I	NO	HS	Runs
437	96	70	4437
Av	100s	1000s	
13.01	-	-	

Bowling career for Surrey:

Balls	Runs	Wkts	Av	Best	5wl
6	6	0			

Catches: 714
Stumpings: 96

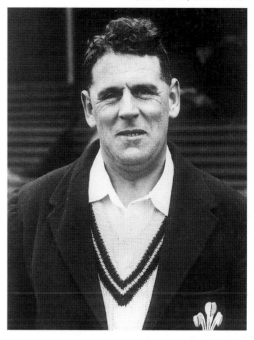

Edward Brooks was the regular wicketkeeper for Surrey between 1928 and 1939. He first joined the county from Cheam CC in 1925 as a medium-pace bowler. He learnt his trade as a professional wicketkeeper by understudying Herbert Strudwick, moved into his position on Strudwick's retirement and became one of Surrey's top stumpers. Brooks took his opportunity splendidly, and became a highly popular figure at The Oval, being a true, good-hearted cockney and a comedian by nature. He was a reliable ally of Alf Gover, taking many catches off his bowling. Standing well back, he would wave first slip away from his right hand because he said that was his area. A big chap, standing 6ft tall, he would throw himself to take catches high or low.

In his career at The Oval, he helped in over 800 dismissals, and his victim per match count was quite high at 2.78. Although a magnificent 'keeper standing back, he failed to maintain this high standard standing up to spinners. Playing against Leicestershire at The Oval, he missed two chances off leg spinner Freddie Brown's bowling in the space of two overs. He followed this by taking a great diving catch to a ball edged low to his right-hand side towards a normal first-slip position off Gover. He then turned to Freddie Brown and said, 'If I can't stump them, I can catch them.' Freddie was not amused.

In his autobiography, *Flannelled Foolishness*, Errol Holmes said of Brooks 'He was a very great-hearted cricketer, one of the best wicketkeepers to fast bowling whom I have ever seen, and what a character!'

Brooks had no pretensions to first-class batting, yet he made 4,504 runs during his career, and could hit or defend dourly as the occasion demanded. He liked the role of nightwatchman at the end of the day, and was far from an easy victim when play resumed. One highlight was when he put on 62 in 50 minutes for Surrey against the Australians, with Alf Gover scoring 62 as they advanced the score from 113 for 9 to the relative respectability of 175 all out.

His benefit year was in 1939, but he did not return to The Oval after the Second World War, although he appeared for the Old England team in the Surrey Centenary Match. In 1940, he played for the London Counties XI against the British Empire XI at Lord's, top-scoring with 50, batting at number nine. For some years after his first-class career ended, Brooks was a licensee at Abingdon, Berkshire, and later became groundsman at Littlehampton Sports Field. He lived at Lyminster, Sussex, in his final years.

A.D. Brown

RHB & LBB (occ. WK), 1992-

Birth: Beckenham, Kent 11/02/1970

Matches: 169 264

Batting career for Surrey:

I	NO	HS	Runs
265	25	295*	10474
254	14	268	7878
Av	100s	1000s	
43.64	32		
32.82	15		

Bowling career for Surrey:

Balls	Runs	Wkts	Av	Best	5wl
816	432	1	432.00	1-56	-
275	261	8	32.62	3-39	-

Catches: 177 83
Stumpings: 1

Tests: 0
ODIs: 16, 1996-1998/99

'Ali' Brown attended Caterham School and played for the various Surrey age groups from Under-11 up to young cricketers. His father played for Surrey Young Amateurs in the 1950s. After a one-day debut in 1991, he made his first-class debut in 1992, scoring three centuries in the season, all in quick time, coming from 79, 71 and 78 balls. He also made his maiden one-day century of 113 against Glamorgan at Llanelli.

Standing 5ft 10in, he is an attacking right-hand bat, commands the crease and uses his strong arms to build a bat speed which sends the ball to the boundary or, often, some way over it. A more mature approach has taught him that major innings require foundations. Originally he bowled leg breaks, but he is now an occasional off-break and medium-pace bowler. An excellent fielder, he specialises being close on the leg side and being an occasional wicketkeeper.

Just as importantly to his team-mates, when those runs have come, never better illustrated than by the fact that in Surrey's two back-to-back County Championship title wins in 1999 and 2000, five of his six centuries have been match-winning efforts. At Oakham School in 2000, Brown showed he had the patience and stamina to match his shot-playing ability, making an unbeaten 295 in eight-and-a-half hours, out of a total of 505, to engineer an innings vic-

tory over Leicestershire. At one stage, Surrey were 190 for 7, but Brown had a tenth-wicket partnership with Saqlain of 141.

He has played for England in 16 one-day internationals, with a highest score of 118 against India in his debut season of 1996, gaining him a reputation as a one-day specialist. This has been helped by holding the record for the highest score recorded in the National League (40 overs) with his innings of 203 off 119 balls scored at Guildford in 1997 against Hampshire in front of the television cameras. In 2002, he smashed the world record for the highest score ever made in a limited-overs match, scoring 268 against Glamorgan at The AMP Oval in the fourth round of the Cheltenham & Gloucester Trophy.

In 1998, he scored a 72-ball first-class century against Northamptonshire at The Oval to share the EDS Walter Lawrence Trophy for the fastest century of the season. In 1999, in the County Championship, he scored 265 against Middlesex at Lord's off 369 balls in 482 minutes.

The manner in which he has scored his runs has made him a favourite with the crowds, a dashing and daring player who can quickly resuscitate a moribund match.

F.R. Brown MBE
RHB & RH or LBB, 1931-1948

Birth: Lima, Peru 16/12/1910
Death: Ramsbury, Wiltshire 24/07/1991

Matches: 106

Batting career for Surrey:

I	NO	HS	Runs
159	16	212	3982
Av	100s	1000s	
27.84	9	0	

Bowling career for Surrey:

Balls	Runs	Wkts	Av
20927	10548	429	24.58
Best	5wI	10wM	
8-34	30	5	

Catches: 68

Tests: 22, 1931-1953

Freddie Brown's career fell into two distinct halves. When he took over at Northampton in 1949, he had had virtually no first-class cricket for nine years, but by 1953, when he finally called it a day in county cricket, he had made 4,331 runs for them and taken 391 wickets.

Before the war, he played for Surrey from 1931 to 1939, and although available for fewer than half their matches, he delighted Oval regulars with his energy and enthusiasm. He had his best and most spectacular season in 1932. In early August, Middlesex, having won the toss, collapsed for 141 and in reply, Surrey were 195 for 5. At this point, Brown, 'in a glorious display of fearless hitting', made 212 in 200 minutes, hitting 7 sixes and 15 fours. His double of 1,135 runs and 120 wickets was rewarded with a trip to Australia with Jardine's 1932/33 side. His talents were scarcely required on this venture, however, and afterwards his County cricket career seemed destined to follow the pattern of many other amateurs – just appearing in a handful of first-class games each season.

Freddie Brown was born at Lima, Peru, where his father, no mean cricketer himself, ran a business. The boy's left-handedness met with paternal disapproval, and he was forced to change over, fortunately with no damage to his natural co-ordination. At his prep school, St

Pirans, he made rapid strides under the tutorage of Aubrey Faulkner so that when he moved on to The Leys School, he had four years of unbroken success with more than 2,000 runs and nearly 200 wickets for the XI. Before his first season at Cambridge, he was advised by Faulkner to concentrate on leg-breaks and googlies as his main weapons in first-class cricket, keeping his medium-pace swingers up his sleeve as a variation. That he was able to carry this out is a tribute to his adaptability. In his two seasons at Cambridge, 1930 and 1931, he exceeded 1,000 runs in 25 matches and took exactly 100 wickets.

During the Second World War, he was a POW for three years and afterwards very little was seen of him. In three seasons, he made one solitary appearance in a Championship match for Surrey. In 1949, he left Surrey with his appointment as captain of Northamptonshire and overnight he was transformed back into the brilliant all-rounder of the early 1930s. He was recalled to the England team and captained them in Australia on the 1950/51 tour.

He was chairman of selectors in 1953, and later in the decade he managed the MCC sides in South Africa and Australia. He was president of the MCC in 1971/72 and was awarded the MBE for his services to cricket.

A.R. Butcher

RHB & LM or SB, 1972-1998

Birth: Croydon, Surrey 07/01/1954

Matches: 284 256

Batting career for Surrey:

I	NO	HS	Runs
481	43	216*	14605
240	24	113*	6051
Av	100s	1000s	
33.34	29	7	
28.01	4		

Bowling career for Surrey:

Balls	Runs	Wkts	Av	Best	5wl
8921	4689	125	37.51	6-48	1
3355	2176	65	33.47	5-19	3

Catches: 130 64

Tests: 1, 1979
ODIs: 1, 1980

After playing for Beckenham Under-11s, Alan Butcher spent five years in Australia, where his family had emigrated. He made a big impression, being selected for the South Australia Under-15 side and later for an all-Australia representative team.

His family returned to England, and Alan played for Surrey Young Cricketers before joining the county staff in 1972, having played two Sunday League games the previous season. Selected primarily as a bowler, he took 6 for 48 against Hampshire at Guildford in his third first-class game. In 1974, his 3 for 11 in the Benson & Hedges Cup semi-final against Lancashire was followed by an eleven-over spell in the final which yielded 23 runs as Leicestershire were beaten by 27 runs. However, the lively left-arm in-swingers were only sparingly used, although some orthodox slow left-arm was occasionally revived in an attempt to break a partnership.

Butcher began opening the batting for Surrey midway through the 1975 season, partnering John Edrich. The following season he achieved his first Championship century, and his consistent batting over the next three seasons earned him an England cap against India at The Oval in 1979. He made 14 and 20, but he was never given another chance at that level, although he was called up for a one-day international against Australia in 1980.

His seasons' aggregates varied between 1,300 and 1,700, on good, bad and indifferent pitches, especially those at The Oval in the mid-1970s, which lacked bounce and pace. He was a well-balanced batsman, the weight evenly distributed on either foot enabling him to launch into a half-volley from the quicker bowlers or position himself for the hook and cut. Most batsmen of small stature and most left-handers favour the latter, and Butcher's trademark was the slash past gully. In 1980, he scored 107 before lunch at The Oval against Glamorgan. Nine years later, on the same ground, he frustrated his former county with a superb defensive innings of 88* that occupied 84 overs.

He hit 1,000 runs in a season twelve times, once going on to 2,000 (2,116, average 58.77, in 1990). In 1987, he left Surrey for Glamorgan and was their captain in the 1989 season. He played against his son in a Sunday League game in 1991. He then returned to Surrey where he is now coach to the Second XI, responsible for developing many of the current First XI cricketers. Over the years, he has shown that he possesses a shrewd cricket brain and the ability to be an inspiring leader.

M.A. Butcher
RHB & RMB, 1992-

Birth: Croydon, Surrey 23/08/1972

Matches: 128 / 44

Batting career for Surrey:

I	NO	HS	Runs
209	19	259	8039
127	25	91	2743

Av	100s	1000s
42.31	15	
26.89	-	

Bowling career for Surrey:

Balls	Runs	Wkts	Av	Best	5wI
6319	3450	104	33.17	5-86	1
2515	2195	49	44.79	3-23	-

Catches: 128 45

Tests: 45, 1997-

With his pedigree, Mark Butcher was always destined to be a cricketer. One uncle, Ian, represented Gloucestershire and Leicestershire, whilst another uncle, Martin, played for Surrey. His father, Alan, played for Surrey for many years, making his debut in the year that Mark was born.

A left-handed opening batsman and medium-paced bowler, Mark won a place on the England Young Cricketers' tour to New Zealand in 1990/91, and made his debut for Surrey in 1991 against a Glamorgan team that included his father in the Sunday League. It was the first time that a father and son had ever played against each other at first-class level.

He was educated at Cumnor House School, Trinity School and finally Archbishop Tenison's School. Although making his first-class debut in 1992, he spent a couple of winters learning his trade in Australia, playing for South Melbourne in 1993/94 and North Perth in 1994/95. His real breakthrough came in 1996, when he scored 1,540 runs in the season and won his county cap. He went to Australia that winter with the England A team and finished with a batting average of over 50, impressing with his judgement, concentration and timing.

Mark Butcher made his Test debut in 1997 against Australia, making a defiant 87 in the second innings. His Test match career has seen ups and downs, but in 45 matches to the end of the 2002 season, he has scored five centuries and 11 fifties. His highest score was 173* against Australia at Headingley in 2001.

This followed a lean spell at the start of the 2000 season, when he had seriously thought of retiring from the game. He fought his way back and the opportunity to play for England came when Hussain was injured and unable to play.

For Surrey, Butcher has formed a formidable opening partnership with Ian Ward. In 2000, they shared a partnership of 359 against Durham at The Oval, leading to an innings victory. He stood in as captain of Surrey in 1999, leading them to five victories as they wrapped up the Championship, hitting a maiden double-century (259) at Leicester. With Nasser Hussain injured, he captained England in the Third Test, but disappointed with the bat and was dropped for the next match on Hussain's return. Runs followed for Surrey in 2001 when he scored another double-century, this time 230 against Glamorgan at Cardiff.

An amiable and intelligent man, he has gained plaudits for his musical ability and The Mark Butcher Band has entertained audiences at several functions.

W. Caffyn
RHB & RM Round-Arm Bowler, 1849-1873

Birth: Reigate, Surrey 02/02/1828
Death: Reigate, Surrey 28/08/1919

Matches: 89

Batting career for Surrey:

I	NO	HS	Runs
154	15	103	3226
Av	100s	1000s	
23.20	23.20	2	

Bowling career for Surrey:

Balls	Runs	Wkts	Av
11539	4299	321	13.39
Best	5wl	10wM	
8-25	29	6	

(plus 10 other wickets)

Catches: 72

Caffyn played his first match for Surrey in 1849, and the following year headed the batting. From that time he never looked back, becoming more and more prominent as the fame of Surrey cricket grew. He was the leading bowler in the team, as well as the finest batsman.

In 1857, he reached his highest point, his best bowling being 9 for 29 playing for Surrey and Sussex against England at The Oval, and until 1863 his powers showed no decline. Then came the end of his main career in English cricket. In the autumn of 1863, he paid his second visit to Australia as a member of George Parr's team, having gone out two years before with H.H. Stephenson's side. At the close of the tour, he stayed behind in the colony, accepting a position as coach. While in Australia he played in inter-colonial matches, but though he did much to develop young talent, he scarcely, judging from the scores, added to his own reputation. He was back in England in 1872 and played several times for Surrey that year. However, in 1873 it was too late to start over again. His long stay in Australia lost him the chance of a benefit match at The Oval, but to the end of his life, the Surrey club paid him an annuity of £39.

On the evidence of all who played side by side with him in his great days, Caffyn was a very fine batsman, free and attractive in style and master of a cut that only Tom Humphrey surpassed in brilliance. Had he lived in these days, he would no doubt have made big scores, for he needed a good wicket. The Oval and Fenner's at Cambridge were the grounds that suited him best. On the rough wickets at Lord's, he was admittedly far inferior to George Parr, Robert Carpenter, Richard Daft, and the first Tom Hayward. Still, even at Lord's against Jackson, he was on two occasions seen at his best. His bowling was basically right-hand medium pace, but he belonged to the purely round-arm school. He had just settled in Australia when the law was altered, and modern wickets would very likely have been too good for him. Still, on the best wickets of his own time, he did wonderful things for Surrey and the United All-England XI. As an all-round fieldsman, he had scarcely a superior.

After his playing career finished, he was a coach at several schools, including Eton, finishing at Haileybury. He settled in Hertford and returned to his trade as a hairdresser.

Birth: Luton, Bedfordshire 05/10/1924
Death: Luton, Bedfordshire 14/06/1981

Matches: 260

Batting career for Surrey:

I	NO	HS	Runs
421	35	191	11458
Av	100s	1000s	
29.68	12	6	

Bowling career for Surrey:

Balls	Runs	Wkts	Av	Best	5wl
5649	2233	73	30.58	5-23	1

Catches: 104

Tom Clark, after heading the Bedfordshire batting averages in 1946, moved to The Oval to join the Surrey staff. His father played cricket for Vauxhall Motors and Tom learned his game at the works club. Whilst with Bedfordshire, he attracted interest from both Surrey and Northamptonshire.

Although he made 74* against Oxford University in 1947 on his first appearance for Surrey, and for three seasons he scored heavily for the Second XI, the county's batting was so strong that it was not until 1950 that he was given a proper trial in the side. That year he made 175* against Cambridge University in five hours. In 1952 he scored 1,000 runs for the first time and was awarded his cap. Until 1959 he remained an essential member of the side, normally opening the innings. His highest score was 191 against Kent at Blackheath in 1956 when he put on 174 in two hours with Peter May for the third wicket. During the Championship-winning years from 1952 to 1959, he scored more runs than anyone else in the side apart from Constable and May, playing in 169 matches, scoring 7,324 runs (average 29.53) with seven centuries, taking 64 wickets (average 25.17) and holding 67 catches.

He played very straight when batting and, unlike some openers, made most of his runs in front of the wicket. He was a useful change off-spinner, a great team man who never grumbled and had the most serene outlook on life. He never moaned if a decision went against him, and always said how lucky he was to play cricket for a living.

Quite early, however, he began to be troubled by arthritis, and, after 1959, he was no longer able to stand the strain of three-day cricket, although he continued for two more seasons to make runs for the Second XI. He was primarily a front-of-the-wicket player and a fine driver. As increasing stiffness stopped him from getting his front foot right out, he took to driving the ball successfully on the rise, a stroke which calls for not only much natural ability but also impeccable technique. With his off-spin bowling in 1952, he took 5 for 23 against Middlesex at Lord's, but with Laker and Eric Bedser in the side, his opportunities were limited. In all first-class cricket, he scored 11,490 runs, with an average of 26.39, including 12 centuries, and took 75 wickets at 30.85 each. Before deciding to concentrate on cricket, he had played professional football for Aston Villa and Walsall.

On his retirement from the game, he lived in Luton and worked for John Oliver, the Buckinghamshire captain, in his agricultural machinery business. During his career, he coached cricket for a time in Argentina.

S.T. Clarke

RHB & RFB, 1979-1988

Birth: Christ Church, Barbados 11/12/1954
Death: Christ Church, Barbados 04/12/1999

Matches: 152 *158*

Batting career for Surrey:

I	NO	HS	Runs
155	18	100*	2130
94	*25*	*45**	*858*
Av	**100s**	**1000s**	
15.55	1	-	
12.43	*-*		

Bowling career for Surrey:

Balls	Runs	Wkts	Av
26783	11226	591	18.99
7855	*4337*	*208*	*20.85*
Best	**5wI**	**10wM**	
8-62	37	6	
5-23	*10*		

Catches: 97 *46*

Tests: [West Indies] 11, 1977/78-1981/82
ODIs: [West Indies] 10, 1977/78-1981/82

Sylvester Clarke was the spearhead of the Surrey attack during the 1980s. He took 85 wickets, average 19.95, in 1982 and was even more impressive in 1988 when he effectively topped the first-class averages with 63 wickets, average 14.49. He was also a very hard-hitting batsman and, in 1981, hit the fastest 100 of the season, in 62 minutes. He missed all of the 1985 season due to injury. His county career was abruptly terminated after a Benson & Hedges match in 1989 for 'persistent breaches of the terms and conditions of his contract'.

Sylvester Clarke played in only 11 Test matches and 6 of those were when West Indies were weakened by the absence of their World Series players. He was an exceptionally fast bowler and in ten years with Surrey rapidly acquired a reputation as perhaps the most feared of them all. He bowled chest-on, his stock delivery zeroing in towards the batsman's body. His bouncer was very hard to pick up, prompting persistent bar-room and dressing-room whispers about its legality. Dennis Amiss called it 'a trap-door ball' because it came out of nowhere. Clarke was canny enough to acquire an out-swinger as well, or at least a ball that held its line.

Clarke began in Barbados with the Kent club where he had watched Charlie Griffith bowl and

made his debut for the island in 1977/78. In his third match, he took a hat-trick against Trinidad and before the season was over was he in the apology for a Test team the West Indies had to field against Australia after the World Series players walked out. He never played another home Test. Before injuring his back, he played in 5 Tests out of 6 in India the following season but suffered from dropped catches. However, he made the full-strength team on tours of Pakistan in 1980/81 and Australia in 1981/82. Standing in the outfield during the first Test staged at Multan, he was pelted by oranges. Cheek-turning not being his custom, he picked up a brick boundary marker and threw it at one of the ringleaders, who was taken to hospital. The game was suspended and so was Clarke. He did visit his victim, but the incident did his long-term prospects no good, and when the West Indian rebels went to South Africa, Clarke signed up. He then built a secondary career playing for Transvaal, Orange Free State and Northern Transvaal in subsequent southern summers, terrorising batsmen there.

Birth: Sidcup, Kent 05/05/1953

Matches: 234 / 74

Batting career for Surrey:

I	NO	HS	Runs
392	50	192	11838
160	13	146	5026

Av	100s	1000s
34.61	20	7
34.19	4	

Bowling career for Surrey:

Balls	Runs	Wkts	Av	Best	5wl
148	192	2	96.00	2-77	-
32	12	0			

Catches: 84 30

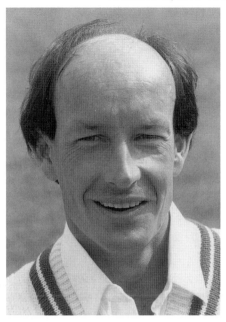

1978 was not a good year for Grahame Clinton. Dropped by Kent after only 4 matches and with competition from Charles Rowe, Bob Woolmer and Graham Johnson for an opening spot, there seemed little prospect of regular first-class cricket. At the age of twenty-five, Clinton could not afford to wait much longer.

1978 was not a good year for Surrey either. Under new captain, Roger Knight, they finished 16th in the County Championship and John Edrich announced his retirement. A new opening bat was required, and Clinton fitted the bill, being left-handed, compact and reliable. In 1979, Surrey finished third in the Champion-ship and were Benson & Hedges Cup finalists. There were many factors to account for the improvement and Grahame Clinton made a crucial contribution with 1,078 runs at an average of 32.78.

At the age of eleven, Grahame Clinton was playing for Kemnal Manor School, then Chislehurst and Sidcup Grammar in Kent, and he made the English Schools team travelling to India in 1970. He was in the company of Alan Butcher, both here and the West Indies in 1972, under the captaincy of John Barclay.

He played senior club cricket, firstly with Sidcup and then Blackheath and, in 1974, he made his debut for Kent. He did not gain a regular place in the team until 1977, when he played 26 matches, and his long and unrewarding apprenticeship led to a chronic lack of self-belief.

On joining Surrey, he received great support from his friend Alan Butcher as his opening partner and Mickey Stewart who had a great hand in developing confidence in his ability, so gaining his cap in 1980. He played in the first team from 1979 to 1990, scoring over 1,000 runs in seven of those seasons and scoring 20 centuries. He made his first century for Surrey against Kent at The Oval. He scored 1,240 runs at 37.57 in 1980, the year he was capped. One of his best seasons was 1985, when he averaged 47.11, although he scored only three centuries. His highest season's aggregate was in 1990, when he scored 1,292 runs at an average of 46.14, but again with only one century. His best score of 192 was against Yorkshire, much earlier in 1984 at The Oval. Grahame Clinton was the star that day. More often than not, he played the supporting role, but always in an uncomplaining way, a true professional. In his first-class career, he totalled 13,118 runs at 33.04.

After his retirement, he was appointed cricket master at Colfe's School in South London, where he also runs a cricket shop. In 1994, he returned to The Oval as chief coach for one season.

B. Constable

RHB & LBB, 1939-1964

Birth: East Molesey, Surrey 19/02/1921
Death: Huntingdon 15/05/1997

Matches: 434 2

Batting career for Surrey:

I	NO	HS	Runs
681	81	205*	18224
2	0	4	4
Av	**100s**	**1000s**	
30.37	26	12	
2.00	–		

Bowling career for Surrey:

Balls	Runs	Wkts	Av	Best	5wl
4888	2585	49	52.75	3-68	

Catches: 174 1

For almost four decades, from 1938 until 1964, the service and commitment of Bernie Constable to Surrey County Cricket was supreme. He made his debut against the West Indies in 1939 as a leg spinner, an ability that was initially seen as his forté rather than the sound, adaptable batsman which he later became. The war interrupted his career which did not really get off the ground again until 1948, after which he gradually became a regular member of the great team of the 1950s. His contributions were often crucial and his commitment never in question. Peter May wrote of him as 'one of those important but unspectacular players on whom most sides rely more than is usually recognised'. These qualities are reflected in his admirable achievement of 1,000 runs in each of 12 seasons, 27 centuries and 18,849 first-class runs at an average of 30.45.

Usually batting at the critical number three position, he adopted a conventional stance from which he produced attractive strokes played all round the wicket in a neat, agile manner. He could score freely, as demonstrated by his highest score (205*) completed in four hours fifty minutes with two sixes and twenty-five fours. His playing of spin bowling on a soft, turning pitch was of a high order. His best season came in 1961, when he was forty, following

surgery to remove a kneecap – he scored 1,799 runs that year. He will be remembered as a fine cricketer and an Oval character.

Although his family were boat builders by the Thames at East Molesey, he was regarded as the epitome of the cock-sparrer Cockney, an image he played up to with his confident strut around the field and his willingness to argue with any-one, including his captain, Stuart Surridge. He would complain loudly if he disagreed with Surridge's field placings.

When not batting, he was always fully involved in the game as one of the most bril-liant, graceful cover-point fielders and as a keen observer of batsmen and bowlers. His captain, Stuart Surridge, said of him: 'He knew exactly where to position himself. He had studied bats-men and knew their strokes so that he stood at just the spot where he knew they would hit the ball. He was a marvellous fielder.'

His loyalty was rewarded with a benefit in 1959, which raised £6,515, a considerable amount which reflected the deeply-felt appreci-ation of members and supporters.

Away from cricket, his sporting prowess extended to golf, in which he became a single handicap player. Before the war, his winters were spent working at Kingston Cricket School run by Surrey team-mates Stan Squires and Tom Barling. After the war and on retirement he worked as a joiner and shopfitter.

Birth: Cane Hill, Surrey 01/12/1886
Death: Epsom, Surrey 02/05/1963

Matches: 120

Batting career for Surrey:

I	NO	HS	Runs
182	22	232	5217
Av	100s	1000s	
32.60	8	3	

Bowling career for Surrey:

Balls	Runs	Wkts	Av
19275	8765	450	19.47
Best	5wI	10wM	
8-24	27	6	

Catches: 74

Tests: 12, 1905/06-1907/08

John Neville Crawford was one of the best all-rounders of his era, although he habitually played in spectacles. He was the son of the Reverend J.C. Crawford and nephew of Major F.F. Crawford, both of whom played for Kent. He created such a reputation as a batsman and a bowler of varying pace at Repton, where he scored 766 runs and took 57 wickets, that he was invited to play for Surrey in 1904 at the age of seventeen.

He was an immediate all-round success, scoring 54 and taking 3 wickets in his first match against Kent during Canterbury week. Moving on to Cheltenham, he and H.C. McDonell bowled unchanged through both innings of Gloucestershire, Crawford taking 10 wickets for 78 and his fellow amateur 10 for 89.

Jack Crawford appeared regularly for Surrey from 1906 until 1909. Twice in succession he completed 'the cricketers' double', being the youngest man at the time to achieve this feat and in 1908 failed to do so a third time by 2 wickets. In fact, he held the most records for the youngest player in the game. In 1908, he made his highest score of 232 against Somerset at The Oval in four hours, including 2 fives and 28 fours. During this period he made 12 appearances for England, going to South Africa in 1905/06 and to Australia in 1907/08 when he headed the Test bowling averages with 30 wickets for 24.79 runs each. After a mid-season dispute with Surrey in 1909, he settled in Australia, playing with distinction for South Australia and paying a visit to New Zealand with an Australian XI in 1914.

Crawford returned to England following the First World War and, with his disagreement having been settled, represented Surrey again from 1919, playing 9 matches, 8 of which were in the Championship until he retired in 1921. A hard-hitting batsman, he shared a match-winning stand of 96 in 32 minutes with Jack Hobbs against Kent in 1919 and the same season played what was described as the innings of his life. Going in at number eight against the Australian Imperial Forces side at The Oval, he hit 144*. When Tom Rushby, the last man, reached the wicket, Surrey needed 45 to avoid a follow-on, but Crawford attacked the bowling with such ferocity that 80 runs were added in 35 minutes. Rushby's share in this partnership amounted to two runs. Of Crawford, *Wisden* recorded: 'The way in which he drove Gregory's fast bowling was magnificent.'

In all first-class cricket, Crawford hit 7,005 runs, average 30.19, dismissed 600 batsmen at a cost of 20.50 runs each and brought off 117 catches.

Birth: Brixton, London 16/02/1886
Death: Lord's, London 23/07/1942

Matches: 422
Batting career for Surrey:

I	NO	HS	Runs
657	59	306*	23108
Av	100s	1000s	
38.64	52	14	

Bowling career for Surrey:

Balls	Runs	Wkts	Av	Best	5wl
1981	903	21	43.00	3-12	-

Catches: 202

Tests: 1, 1921

Andrew Ducat was a productive batsman for Surrey, twice scoring more than 2,000 runs in a season. Naturally a forcing batsman, he used his height, 5ft 10in, in perfect forward strokes. This brought the drive into action with minimal effort. His highest score was 306* against Oxford University at The Oval in 1919, and in that season he scored 1,695 runs at 52.96 placing him sixth in the national batting averages.

A noted soccer player, he appeared for Aston Villa, Southend, Woolwich Arsenal and Fulham and was capped six times for England. He captained Aston Villa to win the FA Cup in 1920. In his youth and subsequently, Andrew Ducat lived at Southend and became a member of The Oval staff in 1906.

An injured knee kept him out of several matches in 1912 and, when football began that winter, a broken leg incapacitated him completely. It seemed that he might be a permanent cripple but a silver plate in the shin bone enabled him to recover so thoroughly that the loss of 1913 preceded a prosperous season. In 1914, he hit four centuries in Championship matches and came out second only to Hobbs in the Surrey averages. For his skill and resolution in playing fast bowling, he was picked for the Headingley Test match against Australia in 1921. However, Ducat still found himself dogged by ill luck, for, in playing McDonald, the shoulder of his bat was broken. The ball went to the slips where Gregory held the catch, while the splinter of wood fell on the stumps shaking off a bail. So Ducat was doubly out in his only Test match.

Again misfortune overtook him at the start of the 1924 season. During net practice, a ball from Hitch fractured a bone in his arm and he could not play during that summer, so he became manager of Fulham FC.

In 1928, Ducat scored 649 runs for twice out in 17 days and made 994 runs in less than six weeks. Ducat maintained his full value as batsman and fieldsman in the Surrey team until the end of the 1930 season. That year he scored 2,067 runs, average 49.21, in all matches, including five centuries, but he fell off next year and, his agreement with Surrey having expired, he was called upon to retire. Altogether in first-class cricket, he scored 23,373 runs at an average of 38.31.

For five years he was a coach at Eton College. During the Second World War he joined the Home Guard. Playing at Lord's for his Surrey Unit against their Sussex brothers-in-arms, he collapsed and died, bat in hand, at the wicket after playing a stroke and waiting to receive another ball.

J.H. Edrich MBE
LHB, 1958-1978

Birth: Blofield, Norfolk 21/06/1937

Matches: 410 /48

Batting career for Surrey:

I	NO	HS	Runs
716	80	226*	29305
143	18	108*	4473
Av	100s	1000s	
46.07	81	18	
35.78	1		

Bowling career for Surrey:

Balls	Runs	Wkts	Av	Best	5wl
49	16	0	-	-	-

Catches: 242 43

Tests: 77, 1963-1976
ODIs: 7, 1970/71-1974/75

John Edrich learned his cricket at his home on a concrete pitch, and his father first bowled to him when he was around the age of five. He was educated at Bracondale Private School, Norwich, and was only fourteen when he played for Blofield Village on Saturdays and South Walsham on Sundays, for whom he hit his first hundreds. In 1954, he played for Norfolk in the Minor Counties and showed sufficient consistency to head their batting averages. A satisfactory trial at The Oval followed and, in 1955, he topped the Surrey batting in the Minor Counties matches.

From the very first day that John Edrich appeared in the nets at The Oval, he attracted criticism for his batting style and over his career he was to become an even more controversial cricketer than his uncle, Bill Edrich. John Edrich appreciated the sound coaching he received, first from Andrew Sandham and later from Arthur McIntyre.

While doing his National Service, he played a fair amount of cricket, but in three appearances for the Combined Services, he failed dismally. Nevertheless, when he returned to The Oval in 1958, he did so well for the Seconds that he was given his first-team chance in the last match against Worcestershire. Surrey were shot out for 57, Edrich with 24* was easily top

scorer, and only one other player reached double figures.

In 1959, Surrey introduced him into the side at Trent Bridge in the middle of May because of injuries to other players. He reached his maiden first-class century in this his second Championship match and he then followed this with another century in the second innings. During his career he scored more than 1,000 runs in a season 21 times, 19 in England and twice in Australia, and in six seasons exceeded 2,000 runs. He scored 103 centuries in his career, and also held the distinction of scoring a century against every other county in the Championship.

Throughout his first-class career, Edrich was involved in 170 century partnerships, 30 of these with M.J. Stewart, 20 with K.F. Barrington and 17 with M.J. Edwards. While Edrich flourished with Surrey, he had a chequered career as an England player. He first appeared for his country against the West Indies in 1963, his six innings yielding only 108 runs. In the following winter, he went to India, but a throat infection kept him out of the first three Tests. Coming into the team for the Second Test in 1964, he achieved the rare and coveted distinction of

hitting a century at Lord's in his first match against Australia. Edrich did little in the next two Tests and, not only was he dropped from The Oval Test, but he was also dropped from the MCC team that toured South Africa.

He was next picked for the third Test against New Zealand in 1965 at Headingley, and celebrated by batting superbly for 310*. Following a good series in Australia in 1965/66, Edrich played in only one match against the West Indies in 1966. During the next few years, he was in and out of the team, but was appointed vice-captain for the tour to Australia in 1974/75. His last Test match was against the West Indies in 1976, when he withstood a battering from the fast bowlers for eighty minutes, taking it on the body when it was impossible to use the bat.

John Edrich was a chunky, strong left-hander, whose success was founded on unwavering concentration, self-discipline and a phlegmatic temperament. He revealed no emotion if struck or beaten by a ball, but would simply take up his stance again and quite likely nudge the next delivery for four as if nothing had happened. His innings did not always live in the memory as being full of beautifully executed shots, but they have endured in the record books and many a lost cause was won because of John Edrich.

In 1973, John Edrich was appointed captain of Surrey in succession to Micky Stewart. At the beginning, things did not go well, but by the end of the season, Surrey finished in second place, 31 points behind Hampshire. In 1974, at the final of the Benson & Hedges, Edrich was presented with the Gold Award by Freddie Brown in recognition of both his solid innings and his tight field settings.

1977 was his last year as captain in the midst of dissension and controversy that was being levelled at the standard of cricket Surrey were providing. The same year, John Edrich hit his 100th century. He was to play one more season after he had resigned the captaincy and then left the game quietly and with dignity whilst still a very good player. He was awarded the MBE in the 1977 birthday honours and lives in retirement on Royal Deeside in Scotland.

Birth: Balham, London 01/03/1940

Matches: 236 *91*

Batting career for Surrey:

I	NO	HS	Runs
415	24	137	10581
87	*7*	*73*	*1441*
Av	100s	1000s	
27.06	12	5	
18.01	*-*		

Bowling career for Surrey:

Balls	Runs	Wkts	Av	Best	5wl
84	34	0	-	-	-

Catches: 262 *27*

Mike Edwards has given lifelong service to the Surrey club. He played for the First XI from 1961 to 1974, and after a career in teaching at an inner London comprehensive school (finishing at Tulse Hill School in Lambeth as deputy head), he became manager of Surrey Young Cricketers from 1980 to 1990. This was followed by his appointment the cricket development officer from 1990 to 1993, director of cricket in 1994 and 1995, and director of cricket development until his retirement in 2002. He was made an honorary vice-president of the club in 2001 and is currently a cricket development consultant.

His father played for Spencer CC and Mike played for them first at the age of fourteen whilst at Alleyns School. He played for Cambridge University from 1960 to 1962 where, surprisingly, he failed to get a Blue, but he did make his first-class debut against Surrey. He was also playing for Surrey Young Amateurs and the Club and Ground sides from 1956, having been a junior member since 1952.

An opening bat, a very occasional off-break bowler and excellent close field, he did not play regularly for the first team until 1964 when he participated in 17 Championship matches with moderate success. In 1965, he was still considered as one of the reserves, but in 1966 he started to open the batting with John Edrich on a regular basis. The move was an instant success and the cultured Edwards, relishing the

extra time and composure he was allowed as an opener, responded with a maiden century against Gloucestershire at The Oval. He scored over 1,000 runs in the season and received his county cap. He then achieved 1,000 runs for five seasons in a row and was a member of the Championship-winning side of 1971, although he missed several games at the end through injury. He retired at the end of the season. In 1967, he headed the national fielding statistics with 53 catches. 1969 was his best batting season when he scored 1,114 runs at 33.75 in Championship games and 1,428 at 36.61 in all matches. During his playing career, he was chairman of the Professional Cricketers' Association from 1970 to 1973.

Mike Edwards played in the domestic one-day matches that started in 1963 and he won the Man of the Match award in the Gillette Cup semi-final against Middlesex in the year when Surrey lost the final to Yorkshire. In his first-class career, he played in 256 matches, scoring 11,378 runs at 26.79 and taking 273 catches. His overseas tours were with the Commonwealth XI to Pakistan in 1967/68 and with the Duke of Norfolk's XI to the West Indies the following winter.

Birth: Balham, London 22/08/1892
Death: Exeter, Devon 15/06/1985

Matches: 414

Batting career for Surrey:

I	NO	HS	Runs
556	52	185	14117
Av	100s	1000s	
28.00	17	4	

Bowling career for Surrey:

Balls	Runs	Wkts	Av
79412	38200	1586	24.08
Best	5wI	10wM	
8-24	86	14	

Catches: 472

Tests: 13, 1920/21-1929

This is the 1930s and Percy George Henry Fender, the Surrey captain and late middle-order batsman, is the centre of attraction, a deceptive-looking cricketer for a big hitter. A tall, slim, six-footer with a pronounced stoop and big horn-rimmed glasses worn only for batting, the 'Skipper' rarely failed his supporters at The Oval. However, his historic fastest hundred, hit in thirty-five minutes, was made at Northampton in 1920.

He was a showman, knowing what the fans expected of him and always willing to take a risk whatever the state of the pitch or quality of the bowling. One of his best knocks at The Oval was against Hampshire in 1922. His 185 included 3 sixes, 3 fives and 24 fours. As a bowler, he was extremely versatile. Essentially a leg-spinner, he could when circumstances called for it, bowl in-swing, out-swing or off-spin. He had an impressive career record of 19,034 runs, 1,894 wickets and 558 catches.

He started his career with Sussex in 1910 and two years later he was in the Gentlemen *v.* Players side at Lord's, but cricket was occupying the whole of his summer, not entirely to his father's approval, who wanted him to go into the family business. His mother was a cricket-

lover and, although agreeing that it was right he should go into business, she stressed that cricket fame could be a useful asset business-wise. So his father found a solution, by asking Fender to move to Surrey as the company was based in London. He became a Surrey player in 1914 and was an instant success, so much so that *Wisden* in 1915 made him one of their Five Cricketers of the Year. After the end of the First World War, he really came into his own; the double of 1,000 runs and 100 wickets in a season being achieved six times in the 1920s.

He captained the county side from 1921 to 1931. He was a kindly man, who was always full of advice and encouragement for the young player, but also a strict disciplinarian who quickly brought players back to even keel if they stepped out of line. He was without a doubt acknowledged as one of the best cricketing brains the game has seen. Leading a Surrey side which, during his career, played at The Oval on one of the best batting strips in the world, he would handle an unbalanced attack so shrewdly that he would often 'fiddle' the opposition batting out. Yet he never led Surrey to a County Championship, although his side was rarely beaten. At one stage, he went 69 matches without defeat before falling to Sussex in 1926.

He always blamed himself for Surrey failing to win the Championship in 1926 when he shared the captaincy with A.C. Wilkinson. In the vital end-of-the-season game against Middlesex at Lord's, and in the side's second innings, Tom Shepherd, batting at number four, was going very well. Fender had a series of signals from the pavilion to his batsmen in the middle. One for 'keep going as you are' and another for 'hurry it up'. He blamed himself because Tom misunderstood the first signal for the latter and, in an attempt to hurry the score along, got himself out. This was the turning point in the game, as the late middle-order batting collapsed and Surrey lost the match.

That particular year was, however, a personal triumph for Percy Fender, as he was the first to perform the cricketing treble of 1,000 runs, 100 wickets and 50 catches in a season.

Another personal triumph was at Lord's when having lost the toss to Middlesex, who batted first, he took 6 wickets in 11 deliveries, including 5 wickets in 7 deliveries. He took a long run for a spinner, 9 loping paces, which he said helped him to get his rhythm and bowl from his full height, getting bounce as well as turn. Useful batting performances include a match at Leicester when Surrey were set 150 to win in 80 minutes. They got them for four wickets, and he hit 91 in 63 minutes, finishing the game off with a six out of the ground. In 1925, at Hove against Sussex, he hit 24 in one over off Maurice Tate, then in his zenith, including 2 sixes. Neighbours Kent had the treatment with a Fender special of 80 in 45 minutes and, near the end of his career, he gave his Oval fans a treat with 139 in 80 minutes against Somerset.

L.B. Fishlock
LHB & SLB, 1931-1952

Birth: Battersea, London 02/01/1907
Death: Sutton, Surrey 25/06/1986

Matches: 347

Batting career for Surrey:

I	NO	HS	Runs
588	41	253	22138
Av	100s	1000s	
40.47	50	12	

Bowling career for Surrey:

Balls	Runs	Wkts	Av	Best	5wl
745	433	9	48.11	4-62	0

Catches: 187

Tests: 4, 1936-1946/47

Laurence Barnard 'Laurie' Fishlock played his first cricket for the All Saints' Choir in Battersea and then in leagues playing in local parks. Whilst at elementary school, he played in representative matches and, after a period at a technical school, he joined a wandering club, Crusaders. He spent seven years working as an engineer before deciding to become a professional sportsman, as a footballer with Crystal Palace. His professional career was later to take him to Millwall, Aldershot, Southampton and Gillingham. Previously as an amateur player he had had considerable success, winning an England cap as a forward.

Once a professional footballer, he found that he could not continue as a full-time engineer, so he had to look for a summer income. Without any recommendation, he wrote to Surrey for a trial and in 1930, he was taken on the staff as a promising left-arm medium-pace bowler. His first-class debut came the following year when he played at The Oval against both Oxford and Cambridge Universities. He spent four seasons with the Second XI and although his bowling did not progress, his batting did, and he began to open the innings. In June 1934, he opened the innings in five first-

class matches, once with his schoolboy hero Jack Hobbs, before dropping down to the middle of the order. Against Somerset at Weston-super-Mare, he almost reached a century scoring 99. He bowled a few overs in most of his 12 matches and took 4 for 62 against Derbyshire at Ilkeston. In all, he took 7 wickets at an average of 23.28 to top the county list.

His maiden century came against Warwickshire at The Oval a year later, a season in which he played in nearly all the county's matches batting at number five, and he received his county cap. In the return match against Warwickshire, he took his ninth and last wicket for the county.

1936 was the year in which he established himself as one of the leading batsmen in England. He topped the Surrey averages and made the most runs. He played in a Test trial match and for the Players against the Gentlemen at Lord's. In July, he made his first of his four Test appearances and, at the end of the season, he was selected to tour Australia and New Zealand. This was an unhappy experience as not only could he not reproduce his domestic form, he also broke a finger at a crucial moment.

In late June of 1937, he was promoted to open the innings for Surrey, a position he was to retain until a year or two before retirement.

In both 1938 and 1939, he was Surrey's leading run-scorer, but with Leyland and Paynter in fine form, he could not regain his England place.

As with all his generation, the war years caused a great gap in his career but as an engineer he remained in London, making parts for the RAF, and so was able to play some cricket. He was selected for the final two matches in the Victory Tests against the Australian Services.

When full-time cricket resumed in 1946, he was thirty-nine, but he quickly showed himself one of the leading batsmen in the country as well as an outstanding fielder. He was selected to play in the Third Test against India at The Oval but made only 8, although he did take the first Indian wicket to fall, his lightning throw from mid-on hitting the stumps. He was one of the last three to be selected to tour Australia and New Zealand and, as before, he had an unsuc-cessful time, again involving a broken bone. His Test career now over, he continued to be Surrey's leading run-scorer until 1951 and in his final season, 1952, he scored 1,000 runs for the county for the twelfth time.

He was essentially a front-of-the-wicket player, driving equally well straight or through the covers but also capable of forcing hard off the back foot. Like so many left-handers he was strong on the leg side, especially in the square-leg area. He was a splendid fielder, especially in the deep. He scored two centuries in a match on four occasions, only Jack Hobbs having exceeded this number. His highest partnership was 260 with Eric Bedser, against Somerset at The Oval in 1949. His career aggregate of 22,138 runs was the seventh highest at the time of his retirement.

He retired whilst still in excellent form and became cricket coach at St Dunstan's School in Catford.

Birth: Sutton, Surrey 06/07/1924

Matches: 300

Batting career for Surrey:

I	NO	HS	Runs
494	40	194	13646
Av	100s	1000s	
30.03	21	4	

Catches: 174

Although joining the staff in 1946, the injury and ultimate retirement of Gregory in 1947 gave an early chance to David Fletcher, then twenty-two years old. He hit four centuries in the course of the season and won rapturous applause from the press and a place in the Players' side against the Gentlemen at Scarborough. Perhaps his best performance was at Bradford, when he carried his bat through the innings for 127 out of 271. His highest score of both the season and his career of 194 came at Trent Bridge against Nottinghamshire. At the Kingston-on-Thames Festival, Fletcher played for the North as one of their players was not fit, and scored 168 against the South. He was never to quite live up to the role which the press would have cast him, but he was a fine player of sound judgement, common sense and a delightful range of shots, particularly on the off.

Partly owing to ill health in 1948, Fletcher failed to maintain his promise of the previous year, but the talent was still there. His only century of the season was 108 against Oxford University at The Oval, although he had several scores over 50 in the Championship. Stuart Surridge believed that David Fletcher

was one of those natural cricketers who failed to follow his own instincts and became a lesser player because of his slavish adherence to the coaching manual. The years from 1949 to 1951 saw him having a lean time with the bat, scoring only two centuries in this period.

By 1952, when enjoying good health for the first time for some years, he lived up to his early promise and formed an opening partnership with Eric Bedser in the first Championship-winning season. An excellent season saw him score 1,674 runs at 38.93 in 25 Championship matches, including 4 centuries. Moreover, Fletcher was most attractive to watch, for his driving and hooking were always crisp and clean.

David Fletcher continued to assist Surrey in their triumphant spell in 1953, scoring 1,381 runs at 32.11 with three centuries. His scores declined in 1954, and the seasons to the end of 1959 saw him maintaining an average in the high twenties.

His form improved considerably in 1960 when he scored 1,259 runs at 35.97 with four centuries, but this turned out to be his last full season as he played in only two Championship matches in his last season, 1961.

Illness and injury reduced his chances of further honours in the game, but he did tour India in 1953/54 with the Commonwealth XI but played in only eight matches. He lives quietly in retirement in Surrey.

A.R. Gover MBE
RHB & RFB, 1928-1947

Birth: Epsom, Surrey 29/02/1908
Death: Putney, London 07/10/2001

Matches: 336

Batting career for Surrey:

I	NO	HS	Runs
386	154	41*	2170
Av	100s	1000s	
9.35	0	0	

Bowling career for Surrey:

Balls	Runs	Wkts	Av
69719	34101	1437	23.73
Best	5wI	10wM	
8-34	87	15	

Catches: 164

Tests: 4, 1936-1946

Encouraged to play cricket by his father, a keen club cricketer, Alf Gover was a fast bowler even at school. When he entered the building trade as a structural engineer, he joined the West Wimbledon Club and through a colleague at work was introduced to the Essex County Club. After a few trial matches he joined Essex and in 1927 travelled to The Oval as twelfth man. A chance conversation with Herbert Strudwick uncovered his Surrey birthplace and this led to him joining his native county for the following season.

He made his debut for Surrey in June 1928, but did not fulfil his early promise until 1930 when he received his county cap. From 1933 until the outbreak of the Second World War in 1939, he was the county's leading wicket-taker and became one of the leading fast bowlers in the country. A tall man for the time (6ft 2½in) with an enthusiastic action, he would charge in, often on totally unresponsive Oval pitches. Although his action was frequently described as cumbersome, at the moment of releasing the ball his left shoulder pointed down the pitch in the orthodox manner so that not only could he produce a vicious break-back, but also the more congenial out-swinger. In 1933 he came to the fore, and the following season saw him twice a

reserve for the Tests against Australia. When, in 1936, he finally played for England against India at Old Trafford, he had the heartbreaking experience of seeing two catches dropped in the slips in his opening spell. During the 1930s, there were many good opening bowlers on the county circuit and most of them played a few times for England without ever commanding a permanent place in the team. Had those two catches been held, he might well have established himself as the leading fast bowler and so filled the vacancy left by the retirement of Harold Larwood.

In 1937, he was selected for the First Test against New Zealand and was then dropped, only to return for the Third Test as a replacement for an original choice. Alf Gover went on the tour to India in 1937/38 with the team captained by Lord Tennyson, but no Test matches were played. He returned to England colours in 1946 at The Oval for what turned out to be his final Test.

That he should have contributed quite so much to the Surrey club could be considered more than a little remarkable as he had been subject to considerable criticism and even ridicule from The Oval crowd as a player. His

very long run, ungainly action and the time taken to bowl an over were always opportunities for the barracker. Yet throughout the second half of the 1930s, he was the Surrey attack and had he been better supported in the slips, he might well have earned the recognition he deserved. It is worth recording the number of wickets he took for Surrey in consecutive years: 116 in 1933, 126 in 1934, 133 in 1935, 179 in 1936, 168 in 1937, 86 in 1938, 129 in 1939, 118 in 1946 and 118 in 1947. He continued to play effectively for Surrey until the age of forty.

In 1938, he took over Strudwick's share in the partnership with Andrew Sandham that ran a cricket school in Wandsworth, and after the war he bought out his partner and spent the next 44 years as a coach. His indoor school in Wandsworth, South London, gained a worldwide reputation and players of all abilities from novices to test stars used the facilities and valued his technical knowledge. He was still coaching in whites until well into his seventies, and many professional cricketers passed through those unprepossessing doors to emerge as better cricketers. Players such as Viv Richards and Andy Roberts were sent to Wandsworth on their arrival in England as budding overseas professionals.

For most of this period, he was on the committee of the Surrey club and in 1980 he was the president. If he was not the greatest cricketer to play for Surrey, few have given longer or more loyal service to the club. It was not until 1998 that Alf Gover received recognition for his services to cricket in the form of an MBE.

Birth: Selsdon, Surrey 26/08/1902
Death: Wandsworth, London 06/10/1973

Matches: 413

Batting career for Surrey:

I	NO	HS	Runs
622	76	243	18978
Av	100s	1000s	
34.75	38	9	

Bowling career for Surrey:

Balls	Runs	Wkts	Av
35987	13877	434	31.97
Best	5wI	10wM	
6-21	11	I	

Catches: 282

Bob Gregory was a valuable all-round cricketer while a professional for Surrey from 1925 to 1947. He was an attractive batsman who, being rather a small man, was stronger off the back foot than the front. He scored 19,495 runs at an average of 34.32, with leg-break bowling took 437 wickets and held 281 catches. In addition, he had few equals in his day as a deep fieldsman. He reached 1,000 runs in nine seasons. Of his 39 centuries, the highest was 243 against Somerset at The Oval in 1938.

He first made his mark in 1926 with a century against Hampshire at Southampton and, by 1928, his bowling was proving most effective. He made a notable advance in his batting and was displaying considerable promise. In 1932, he scored three Championship centuries and, in 1933, achieved 1,000 runs for the season.

As the playing career of Jack Hobbs neared its end, 'Bob' Gregory often opened the county innings in his place and in 1934 he scored 2,379 runs, including eight hundreds, average 51.71. He opened the batting with Andy Sandham and, as a fielder, he was in a class of his own to such an extent that he was called up to act as twelfth man for England. In 1935, a new lbw law was introduced, and Gregory's form and confidence were so badly affected that towards the end of the season he was actually dropped. It was said at the time that he was never quite so good thereafter, but he still managed 2,166 runs with seven centuries at an average of 46.08 in 1937. He scored more than 1,000 runs per season from 1936 to 1939 and in 1947. In Sandham's last match against Sussex at Hove, Gregory shared a partnership with him of 167. In 1938, his opening partner was Laurie Fishlock.

Popular with players and spectators alike, Gregory went to India with Jardine's MCC team in 1933/34. Although he did not gain a place in the side for any of the three Test matches, he hit 148 against the Bombay Presidency. He gave up playing in the middle of the 1947 season, chiefly owing to knee trouble, at the age of forty-four having helped Surrey re-establish themselves in their first post-war season. He made 1,440 runs in his last full season.

In his early days, he played football for both Norwich and Fulham. After leaving Surrey, he became secretary of Watney Mann's Sports Club on Errol Holmes' recommendation. In this job, he found a new and rewarding life among sportsmen of several kinds, with whom he was very popular, so much so that he was persuaded to stay on until he died in harness, aged seventy-one.

Birth: Ripley, Surrey 20/12/1833
Death: Stoke-next-Guildford, Surrey 03/05/1879

Matches: 165

Batting career for Surrey:

I	NO	HS	Runs
288	15	142	4604
Av	100s	1000s	
16.86	2		

Bowling career for Surrey:

Balls	Runs	Wkts	Av
22509	9125	548	16.65
Best	5wI	10wM	
9-130	44	7	

Catches: 139
Stumpings: 2

Not without cause has the poet sung: 'If George Griffith gets a loose one, he will send it far away.' By common consent, he was the hardest hitter known until the time of C.I. Thornton. Caffyn considered him the best left-handed batsman there had been, with the possible exception of Felix. By 1864, Griffith was not only the most powerful hitter in the game but he was also one of the quicker bowlers, yet not averse to contrasting his round-arm quick bowling with some telling slow lobs, at times in the same match. On occasions, however, his bowling was extremely nasty.

A baker by trade, he joined the staff at The Oval in 1857, the year after he left the Priory Park Club in Chichester, but he then left Surrey at the end of the 1863 season because of a disagreement over terms. This did not preclude him from playing for the County and he continued to assist them until 1872. In 1864, it was his 6 for 32 which did much to bring Surrey their first victory of the season against Oxford University at The Oval in mid-June. The previous three days had seen Surrey draw their second county match, at Sheffield.

His best performance was his 89 and 142 against Sussex in 1862, but his scoring throughout the fifteen years he played for the county was consistently high. At Hastings in August 1864, playing for the United All England XI against 22 of Hastings and St Leonards, he hit George (Farmer) Bennett for four consecutive sixes in a four-ball over, each hit being sent out of the ground for distances exceeding 100 yards. Playing in the Gentlemen and Players match at The Oval in 1861, he hit the ball clean out of the ground.

Between 1856 and 1871, at a time when county fixtures were still relatively scarce, he captured 600 wickets for Surrey. Three times in his career, he bowled unchanged throughout a county match. His best bowling performance was 9 for 130 for Surrey against Lancashire at The Oval in 1867. He went on two overseas tours, firstly with Stephenson to Australia in 1861/62 and then with Willsher to North America in 1868. At one time he was called 'The Lion' when in a competition in Australia he threw a cricket ball over 120 yards. Surrey awarded him a benefit in 1872 and *Wisden* commented: 'Surrey's committee never granted The Oval to a worthier fellow, a more popular professional or harder working cricketer.'

After retiring from the game, he was in demand as a coach being engaged in 1873 by Oxford and Rugby, then in 1874 by Oxford, Winchester and Harrow and in 1875 by Oxford and Cheltenham.

E. G. Hayes
RHB & LBB, 1896-1919

Birth: Peckham, London 06/11/1876
Death: West Dulwich, London 02/12/1953

Matches: 500

Batting career for Surrey:

I	NO	HS	Runs
802	45	276	25062
Av	100s	1000s	
33.10	45	16	

Bowling career for Surrey:

Balls	Runs	Wkts	Av
25125	12761	473	26.97
Best	5wI	10wM	
8-22	12	2	

Catches: 560

Tests: 5, 1905/06-1912

Ernie Hayes learnt his cricket at East Dulwich College, played for Honor Oak CC and joined the groundstaff at The Oval in 1895. He made his first appearance for Surrey the following year and ended his first-class career some thirty years later. His first match for the county was against Australia, when he scored 62 in two and a half hours against Jones at his fastest. He had few opportunities in 1897 and a disappointing season in 1898, but the turning point came against Australia in 1899 when scoring 131 he helped Surrey to victory by 104 runs. In his career, he scored 27,325 runs, average 32.18, hitting 48 centuries; with leg-breaks, he took over 500 wickets, and held 605 catches.

His most successful season as a batsman was that of 1906 when he scored 2,309 runs, average 45.27, and reached three figures on seven occasions. The highest of his 48 centuries was 276 against Hampshire at The Oval in 1909, when he and Hobbs shared in a wonderful second-wicket stand of 371.

Especially strong in driving, he also pulled fearlessly, had a variety of strokes and was always attractive to watch. One of the best and safest of slips, he did good work in the deep and was by no means to be despised as a bowler. In 1909, he made his only Test match appearance against Australia, although he had toured that country with A.O. Jones's side two years previously. He played four times for England against South Africa, three when touring the Union in 1905 and the other at home in 1912. He represented Players against Gentlemen on many occasions, being captain at The Oval in 1914.

Until the First World War, in which he served with the 30th Royal Fusiliers, he played regularly for Surrey, but after re-appearing as an amateur he left the county in 1919. Damaged hands contributed to his decision to retire, having fielded in the slips to Tom Richardson and Bill Lockwood in their prime. This caused his fingers to curl up as the nerves were put out of action by frequent bruising and left him having difficulty in gripping a bat. Nevertheless, in his last season for Surrey he scored 153 against Hampshire at Southampton, adding 353 in a third-wicket partnership with Ducat which lasted 165 minutes.

From Surrey he went to Leicestershire as coach, taking part in matches for the Second XI with such success, that, in 1926, he was persuaded to turn out for the Championship side. At the age of fifty, he headed the Leicestershire averages, scoring 254 runs at an average of 36.28 and failing by one run to complete a century against Nottinghamshire at Trent Bridge. He returned to The Oval in 1929 as coach, a position he held until 1934, when he became a licensee in West Norwood.

Copyright
PHOTO HAWKINS BRIGHTON.

Birth: Cambridge 29/03/1871
Death: Cambridge 19/07/1939

Matches: 593

Batting career for Surrey:

I	NO	HS	Runs
932	79	315*	36171
Av	100s	1000s	
42.40	88	20	

Bowling career for Surrey:

Balls	Runs	Wkts	Av
17831	9342	436	21.42
Best	5wl	10wM	
8-89	17	2	

Catches: 420

Tests: 35, 1895/96-1909

Tom Hayward was one of the greatest batsmen of all-time. A son of Daniel Hayward, a player of some repute, he was also a nephew of Thomas Hayward, who in the 1860s was by common consent the leading professional batsman in England. Both his father and grandfather appeared in the Surrey XI. His family lived for many generations in Mitcham.

Like his famous uncle, he played with beautiful style. Using a straight bat, he possessed all the qualities essential for success at the wicket: unlimited patience, admirable judgement, watchfulness and strong defence. While he scored all round the wicket, his chief strokes were the cut and off-drive. It may be questioned whether anyone ever surpassed him in making the off-drive, the stroke being executed delightfully and so admirably timed that the ball was rarely lifted. Of good height and build, Hayward had remarkable powers of endurance. He first appeared for Surrey in a county match in 1893, when he batted at first wicket down, and he was promoted to open the innings in 1900. In 1898, he played his greatest innings of 315* against Lancashire at The Oval.

Equal in merit was his 130 for England when badly needed against Australia at Old Trafford in 1899. At The Oval in the same season, Hayward and F.S. Jackson, the best batsmen in the earlier Tests, were chosen by to open the England innings and they made 185, the amateur's share being 118. Hayward played in 29 Tests against Australia, which he visited three times, and also played six matches against South Africa. An automatic choice for the Players, Hayward, in 29 matches against the Gentlemen, scored 2,374 runs with an average of more than 47.

For twenty years in succession, from 1895 to 1914, he scored over 1,000 runs each season. In 1904, he made 3,170, and in 1906 he scored 3,518 runs, which stood as the record aggregate in first-class cricket until 1947 when surpassed by Denis Compton. Hayward (273) and Abel (193) created a world partnership record for the fourth wicket with 448 against Yorkshire at The Oval in 1899. Before the First World War, Hayward and Hobbs became the most notable opening pair in the game, sharing in 40 century partnerships. In 1907, they accomplished a performance without parallel by making 100 for Surrey's first wicket four times in one week: 106 and 125 against Cambridge University at The Oval, followed by 147 and 105 against Middlesex at Lord's.

Hayward was the first batsman after W.G. Grace to complete 100 centuries and altogether he reached three figures on 104 occasions, 58 times at The Oval. In three matches he scored a hundred in each innings, excelling in 1906 by doing this twice in six days – 144* and 100 at Trent Bridge off the Nottinghamshire bowlers, 143 and 125 at Leicester. At Nottingham, he carried his bat through the first innings, the next highest score being 32. In that season, he made 13 centuries, equalling the record set by C.B. Fry in 1901. Eight times he carried his bat through an innings, and he achieved the double in 1897 with 1,368 runs and 114 wickets. He also scored 1,000 runs before the end of May in 1900.

When at the height of his fame as a batsman, Tom Hayward was also worth his place as a bowler. In 1897, Tom Richardson took 238 wickets at 14.55, Hayward coming next with 91 at 19.28. Hayward, bowling medium-paced off-breaks, contrasted with Richardson, whose expresses often whipped back from off to leg stump. Leicestershire experienced the strength of this combination in 1897 on the Aylestone Road ground when they were twice dismissed for exactly the same total, 35. Hayward took 7 wickets for 43 and Richardson 12 for 20. They bowled unchanged in each Leicestershire innings and the match was all over in a day. Between the two collapses, Surrey made 164, Hayward being top scorer with 26. In 1899, Hayward twice performed the hat-trick, against Gloucestershire at The Oval and Derbyshire at Chesterfield.

Putting on weight, he became rather slow in the field, although he continued to play until the end of the 1914 season. He did not attempt to return to cricket when it resumed after the war in 1919. In his first-class career, Tom Hayward scored 43,409 runs at 41.69 and took 481 wickets at a cost of 22.94 each.

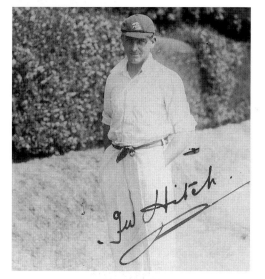

Birth: Radcliffe, Lancashire 07/05/1886
Death: Rumney, Cardiff 07/07/1965

Matches: 305

Batting career for Surrey:

I	NO	HS	Runs
423	41	107	6765
Av	100s	1000s	
17.70	3		

Bowling career for Surrey:

Balls	Runs	Wkts	Av
50571	26550	1232	21.55
Best	5wI	10wM	
8-38	90	21	

Catches: 202

Tests: 7, 1911/12-1921

A firm favourite at The Oval, where he was loved as much for his big hitting and brilliant fielding as for his bowling, Bill Hitch was a devoted cricketer, who always displayed tremendous energy and enthusiasm. He played his first serious cricket with Cheveley, just south of Newmarket. Recommended by Tom Hayward, he joined The Oval staff in 1905 and made his debut in 1907. He soon established himself as one of the fastest bowlers in the country. He had an unusual hesitant run-up in which his approach to the crease was punctuated by two or three hops. More than once, he broke a stump and at The Oval, in 1921, he sent a bail 55 yards and 1 foot when bowling A.R. Tanner of Middlesex.

His most successful season was that of 1913 when he took 174 wickets at 18.55 each, including 8 for 48 in an innings at The Oval against Kent, that year's Champions. He represented Players against Gentlemen ten times, taking three wickets in four balls on his final appearance at The Oval in 1923. He achieved the hat-trick on two occasions, first against Cambridge University in 1911, when taking four wickets in five balls, and then against Warwickshire in 1914, both at The Oval.

He toured Australia with MCC in 1911/12 and 1920/21 without marked success, playing for England on both tours as well as appearing in Tests in England in 1912 and 1921. Against Australia at The Oval in 1921, he scored one of the fastest innings recorded in Test cricket – 51* in 40 minutes. Always a spectacular hitter, he more than once hit a ball clean out of The Oval. At Trent Bridge in 1919, he scored 74 out of 84 balls in 35 minutes and against Glamorgan at The Oval in 1924, he received only 12 balls when scoring 32 in 17 minutes. In his benefit match against Kent at The Oval in 1921, he reached 71 in 50 minutes.

In any position he fielded magnificently. Hitch was quite outstanding at short-leg, where he stood often perilously close to the bat. In his first-class career, the highest of his three centuries was 107, hit in 70 minutes, against Somerset at Bath in 1922.

From 1926 to 1929, he was a professional with Todmorden in the Lancashire League where his younger brother, R. Hitch, was an amateur with Rawtenstall. Todmorden won the Championship once and were twice runners-up. He took 289 wickets at 11.62 each, one of his best performances being 8 for 45 against Rishton in 1927.

He was a first-class umpire (1932-36), standing in four Test matches (including three in India in 1933/34). He later became coach to Glamorgan before taking a position with a South Wales firm, for whom he played in annual matches until he was well over sixty.

Sir J.B. Hobbs

RHB & RMB, 1905-1934

Birth: Cambridge 16/12/1882
Death: Hove, Sussex 21/12/1963

Matches: 598

Batting career for Surrey:

I	NO	HS	Runs
956	80	316*	43554
Av	100s	1000s	
49.71	144	24	

Bowling career for Surrey:

Balls	Runs	Wkts	Av	Best	5wl
3844	1948	86	22.65	7-56	3

Catches: 241

Tests: 61, 1907/08-1930

Jack Hobbs is a strong candidate for the greatest batsman ever, with a career that was interrupted by the First World War but still resulted in 199 centuries. This total includes two centuries scored in India in 1930/31, in matches that were subsequently classified as first-class by the Association of Cricket Statisticians and Historians.

He became the consummate opening batsman, with a solid defence and a powerful attacking game, showing mastery of most strokes. Hobbs was known as one of the best runners between wickets in the game, especially with his regular opening partners of Hayward and Sandham for Surrey and Sutcliffe for England. He was remarkable in his ability to play high quality bowling on bad pitches, especially Australian sticky wickets. He was also a splendid fielder, running out many from his favoured position in the covers and a respectable fast-medium change bowler.

He had all the gifts of a great batsman. They included the qualities of understanding and sensitivity to a degree that made him unique. Others scored faster, hit the ball harder, but no one else batted with more skill than he, which was based on an infallible sympathy with the bowled ball. His great achievements were recognised in 2000, when selected by *Wisden* as one of the Five Cricketers of the Century.

John Berry (Jack) Hobbs was the eldest of the twelve children of John Cooper Hobbs and Flora Berry. His father was a professional at Fenner's and later groundsman at Jesus College. Jack Hobbs received no formal coaching, but he would get up at six to practise on Parker's Piece in Cambridge. Tom Hayward was a particular hero of Jack Hobbs' and was partly responsible for bringing him to Surrey's notice. His promise earned him a trial with Surrey in 1903, after Essex had ignored his application.

Surrey gave Hobbs an immediate opportunity as soon as he was qualified, and in his first match against the Gentlemen of England in 1905, he made 18 and 88. He was awarded his county cap when he followed this with 28 and 155 against Essex in his first Championship game. He married Ada Ellen in September 1906 and they had four children – Jack, Leonard, Ivan and Vera.

In 1907, he scored 0 and 1 against Nottinghamshire, the nearest he ever came to 'bagging a pair'. He went to Australia in 1907/08 and made his debut at Melbourne, scoring 83, and until his Test career ended in 1930, England never omitted him when he was available. All but 2 of his 61 Tests were against Australia and South Africa. By 1909, Hobbs

had established his authority in all English conditions, and he completed his apprenticeship when, in 1909/10, he faced South Africa's battery of spin bowlers on matting wickets. At Melbourne in 1911/12, against Australia, he and Wilfred Rhodes set a record of 323 for the first wicket when England went on to win the series. In 1914, Surrey were Champions for the only time in his career when he made 11 centuries, 3 of them over 200.

At this stage in his career, Hobbs had scored 25,587 runs, with 65 centuries. The war years could have been his prime, and at thirty-six he would not be certain of recovering his old ascendancy. But, in the event, all these figures were to be more than doubled. By his retirement in 1934, he had made 61,760 runs, at an average of 50.70, including 199 centuries, 100 of them being scored after his fortieth birthday.

Hobbs showed much of the old aggression in 1919, but in 1921 a muscle injury was followed by an ulcerated appendix which nearly cost him his life. Adapting his style to his physical limitations, he now dominated the bowlers off the back foot. In 1925, he scored 10 of his 16 centuries in the first 12 games, and he led the English averages with 3,024 runs at 70.32. The following year, his 316* for Surrey was the highest innings ever played at Lord's at that time. In the final Test at The Oval, a masterly century on a turning wicket helped to recover the Ashes from Australia. In 1928, he had an average of 82 and went to Australia for the last time the following winter.

In his career, he shared in 166 century opening partnerships, an average of one every eight innings, the highest being 428, with a total of 302 century partnerships for all wickets, an average of one in 4.5 innings. On six occasions, he made two centuries in one match, and he scored centuries both home and away against every county.

With the proceeds of his benefit in 1919, Hobbs opened a sports shop in Fleet Street in which he continued to take an active interest after he left the game. Surrey made Jack Hobbs a life member in 1935, and his knighthood in 1953 was the first conferred on a professional cricketer. The Hobbs Gates at The Oval and a pavilion on Parker's Piece stand as tangible memorials of his career.

Birth: Battersea, London 10/02/1876
Death: Crystal Palace, London 05/02/1957

Matches: 282

Batting career for Surrey:

I	NO	HS	Runs
425	29	171	10323
Av	100s	1000s	
26.06	12	4	

Bowling career for Surrey:

Balls	Runs	Wkts	Av	Best	5wl
917	570	13	43.84	2-20	-

Catches: 232

Frederick Holland played as a batsman for Surrey from 1894 to 1908, scoring 10,384 runs in all first-class matches, including 12 centuries, at an average of 25.57. Four times he exceeded 1,000 runs in a season. Encouraged by seven of his eight brothers, he played cricket from the early age of three, playing club cricket for Advance and Oxalis Clubs of Battersea. In 1892, he wrote to Surrey authorities for a trial which he was given and as he proved eminently satisfactory, he became a member of the groundstaff at The Oval in 1893, when just seventeen years old.

At 6ft tall, he had a graceful and commanding style, showing a special advantage in cutting and hitting to leg, and he was a very good short slip. He was a big hitter on occasions and when playing for the Club and Ground or Second XI was known to hit the ball out of the ground at The Oval.

After a very successful spell in the Second XI, he played twice for the first team in 1894, his scores including 31* against the first South African team and 76 against Essex at Leyton. In 1895, his first innings was 123 against Essex and he latter recorded his highest innings of 171 against Cambridge University, both at The Oval. In the Cambridge match, he and Abel (165) added 306 for the third wicket. This form antici-

pated a high place in the world of cricket but he never fully realised these expectations.

For the first few weeks of 1895, he could do no wrong, batting in superb style but a sprained arm kept him out of the XI for some time. In that season, he scored 832 runs at 33.28 in twenty-five completed innings and contributed in no small degree to Surrey's success in winning the Championship that year. He was an excellent servant for Surrey, scoring 1,000 runs in a season in four years, 1898, 1903, 1905 and 1907. In 1896, he hit 153 from the Warwickshire bowling at Edgbaston.

He made one appearance for the Gentlemen against the Players at The Oval in 1904. In the winter of 1898/99, he went to South Africa as a professional with the Union Club of Port Elizabeth for the season. Frederick Holland possessed a good baritone voice, for some years singing at cricket concerts and also making appearances on the music hall stage, to the extent that he considered making it a career when he finished playing. In the First World War, he served in the Army Service Corps. Following his retirement from first-class cricket, he became coach at Oundle School.

A.J. Hollioake
RHB & RFMB, 1993-

Birth: Melbourne, Australia 05/09/1971

Matches: 134 206

Batting career for Surrey:

I	NO	HS	Runs
205	18	208	7823
178	25	117*	4252
Av	100s	1000s	
41.83	15	2	
27.79	2		

Bowling career for Surrey:

Balls	Runs	Wkts	Av	Best	5wl
7297	4065	102	39.85	5-62	1
6637	5983	272	21.99	5-29	21

Catches: 131 64

Tests: 4, 1997-1997/98
ODIs: 35, 1996-1998/99

After the tragic death of his brother, Ben, in March 2002, Adam stayed in Australia with his family until mid-season. On his return, he led Surrey to their third Championship title in four years, and those who know him well recognised changes in his personality. He was less combative and more understanding.

Adam Hollioake was born in Melbourne, Australia, and went to school in Sydney at St Joseph's College, and then St Patrick's College in Ballarat. His third school was in England, St George's, Weybridge, from which he went to Surrey Tutorial College in Guildford. He played for Surrey Young Cricketers, touring Australia with them. Adam then went to New Zealand with England Young Cricketers in 1990/91 and played for Fremantle in Western Australia that same winter.

Standing 5ft 11in tall, he is a right-hand batsman and a right-arm medium-fast bowler. After some games for the Surrey Second XI in 1991, he qualified for England in 1992 by residency and made his county debut the same year in a one-day match. He made a sensational first-class debut for Surrey, scoring 13 and 123 v. Derbyshire at Ilkeston in 1993. With his best bowling figures to date of 4-22 v. Yorkshire at The Oval, he was awarded his Surrey cap in 1995. He scored 1,522 first-class runs in 1996 and played in two limited-overs internationals for England, taking 4 for 23 on this debut v. Pakistan at Edgbaston.

His 39 wickets in the Sunday League in 1996 smashed the previous best League record (34). Adam toured Australia in 1996/97 as the England A captain. He achieved the amazing record of not only being at the wicket when England won all three games, but actually hitting the winning runs as England triumphed by the same margin in each fixture. Adam and his brother Ben became the first brothers to make their Test debut together in the twentieth century in the Fifth Test against Australia at Trent Bridge in 1997. Adam has so far played in only four Test matches.

He went to Sharjah as England ODI captain for the Champions' Trophy in 1997/98, followed by trips to the West Indies, Bangladesh, Australia and Sharjah. He played for England in the 1999 World Cup. As an accomplished all-rounder, he has produced many valuable performances for Surrey at critical times, both in the first-class and one-day game. In 2002, he made his highest score of 208 against Leicestershire at The Oval. One of his strengths is his enthusiasm and this has helped him to be a successful leader, becoming captain of Surrey in 1997 and taking them to three Championship triumphs in 1999, 2000 and 2002.

E.R.T. Holmes
RHB & RFMB, 1924-1955

Birth: Calcutta, India 21/08/1905
Death: Marylebone, London 16/08/1960

Matches: 198

Batting career for Surrey:

I	NO	HS	Runs
298	40	206	8837
Av	100s	1000s	
34.25	15	5	

Bowling career for Surrey:

Balls	Runs	Wkts	Av	Best	5wl
11869	6135	173	35.46	6-16	3

Catches: 145

Tests: 5, 1934/35-1935

Errol Holmes was one of the most gifted amateur batsmen of his day. He soon showed an aptitude for cricket at Andrew's School, Eastbourne, before becoming one of the greatest cricketers Malvern has produced. He went up to Oxford, promptly gaining his Blue and for three seasons was a prominent member of the side, being captain in his last year. He also gained his association football Blue as a centre forward, and in due course captained the side. Although he had one or two triumphs with his medium-fast bowling, it was with his batting that Holmes made such a fine impression on his introduction to first-class cricket. For Oxford, against the Army, he scored 238 runs for once out, scoring 553 in the season, average 34.56.

A marked characteristic of his batting was the ease and certainty of his strokes. A very strong forward player, he drove really hard, especially to the off and so good was his footwork and power of wrist that he had no need to exploit the modern method of leg-side play. Nevertheless, he was no mean exponent of such strokes. With left shoulder forward and firm right knee, Holmes convinced one directly he went in that he was there to make runs. He never did change his method.

His first match for Surrey in 1924 was against Somerset at Taunton, where he failed to score, but the following year he took part in the his-

toric 'Hobbs' match. On leaving university, Holmes, due to business reasons, dropped out of first-class cricket for seven years, but the break did not harm his batting. He returned to Surrey (1934) at a time when the affairs of the club were unsettled and was captain from 1934 to 1938. He entertained the idea that County cricket required some vitalising influence. He applied himself to the task of installing the precepts of the country house spirit into the minds and consequently the play of those under him. For a few seasons he was undoubtedly one of the best batsmen of his day. Scoring 1,925 runs, he finished tenth in the national batting averages in 1935 and played in the Second Test against South Africa at Lord's. He was vice-captain of the MCC team which went to the West Indies in 1934/35 and the following winter he led the side to Australia and New Zealand on a goodwill tour.

Again in 1936 he was in fine form and was chosen to go with MCC to Australia in 1936/37, but his business interests compelled him to decline. He announced his retirement from first-class cricket in 1938, but after the war when Surrey were again hard-pressed for a responsible leader, he returned as captain in 1947 and 1948. From 1949 to 1953, he was a member of the MCC committee.

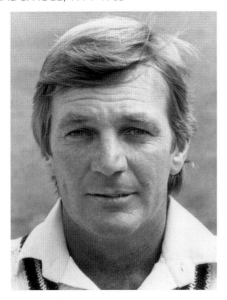

Birth: Auckland, New Zealand 29/03/1951

Matches: 188 *169*

Batting career for Surrey:

I	NO	HS	Runs
323	25	183	9284
160	*4*	*122*	*3765*
Av	100s	1000s	
31.15	18	3	
24.13	*2*		

Bowling career for Surrey:

Balls	Runs	Wkts	Av	Best	5wl
1662	848	16	53.00	3-20	-
123	*110*	*7*	*15.71*	*4-16*	*1*

Catches: 109 *47*

Tests: [New Zealand] 47, 1974/75-1984/85
ODIs: [New Zealand] 70, 1974/75-1984/85

In 1969, at the age of eighteen, Geoffrey Howarth arrived in England to join the Surrey staff as a batsman of promise and an occasional off-spinner. He spent fourteen years at The Oval and was recognised amongst his team-mates as an immensely talented batsman. He was one of three overseas players on the staff when, at that time, only two could play in any one match for the first team. The other two were Intikhab Alam and Sylvester Clarke, so team selection depended on the wicket conditions. Howarth missed out on several occasions, but accepted the situation stoically.

He was nicknamed 'Old Bones' as his colleagues considered he would never make old bones because he was always nursing some strain or pull. It was said that his technique as a batsman contributed to his failings. He thrived on good, true pitches and in Australia he was successful as a big scorer. His tendency to play across the line did lead to his undoing in English conditions. On his day, he was a dominant batsman who could destroy an attack and was an excellent judge of run-rate. He was captain of Surrey in 1984 and 1985.

As a person and as a professional, Geoff changed dramatically over the years. Originally, he was something of a rebel, and when told to wear a collar and tie at The Oval he asked 'Why, will it make me hit the ball through the covers better?' He then did not appear very pleased

when somebody told him that it would! It was pointed out that if he became a more disciplined person with more regular habits and way of life, he may also begin to be sharper and more disciplined in the way he put an innings together and be generally more efficient and less lackadaisical in his game. Geoff was actually sacked from The Oval one September and was taken back on the staff again the following Spring. From that moment, his attitude and technique improved enormously.

Geoff became a good County player and then a fine Test player, at times even a great Test player. His knowledge of batting extended to the rest of cricket and he achieved his just reward in being made captain of his country. He became the most successful captain ever for New Zealand and was very deservedly awarded first the MBE, and then an OBE for his services to New Zealand cricket. Richard Hadlee commented that all the New Zealand team regarded him as having something very special to offer the team as captain.

Geoff is a very likeable man with a marvellous sense of humour which was very necessary when considering some of the predicaments that he found himself in. Now retired, he splits his time between England and his native New Zealand.

Birth: Hoshiarpur, India 28/12/1941

Matches: 232 *185*

Batting career for Surrey:

I	NO	HS	Runs
338	45	139	5707
159	*29*	*62*	*2439*

Av	100s	1000s
19.47	4	0
18.76	*0*	

Bowling career for Surrey:

Balls	Runs	Wkts	Av
38701	18871	629	30.00
5739	*3867*	*131*	*29.51*

Best	5wI	10wM
8-74	25	2
6-25	*3*	

Catches: 73 *38*

Tests: [Pakistan] 47, 1959/60-1976/77
ODIs: [Pakistan] 4, 1972/73-1976/77

In an era when there was so much adverse criticism in relation to the employment of too many overseas cricketers, Surrey will always look back with pleasure on their first such appointment. Possibly one might say that Intikhab had not made the same impact on the county scene as several of his contemporaries, yet he brought to Surrey so many other ingredients and no other overseas player displayed more loyalty over twelve years.

Pakistan's leading cricketer was not pushing for an exorbitant contract, but was merely content to be accepted on similar terms to his new-found colleagues. He was accepted in every possible way and within a matter of weeks his cheerfulness, his intense love of the game and his hard-working skills had made him a most popular member of the side. Being able to play cricket every day of the week, he reached the highest echelon of leg-break bowlers at a time when they were fast becoming a dying breed and seldom did he find conditions suitable for him.

It speaks volumes for his total unselfishness and team spirit that, much against the grain, he had once more to adapt his own bowling to met the needs of his side. The leg spinner has always been an attacking bowler and wickets are often bought expensively, but cricket's new format now put the emphasis on containment. There is no question that 'Inti' was born thirty years too late. How Percy Fender would have welcomed him in his side! As a genuine wrist spinner and powerful middle-order batsman, he would have raced to the double in the mid-1930s, and conditions that abounded in those days in Australia and West Indies would have been made to measure for him.

With so little in his favour, it is remarkable that he achieved so much. For Surrey alone, he took 629 wickets, scored 5,707 runs and all his four centuries were well worth watching. At international level, he appeared in 47 Test matches, taking 125 wickets and becoming the first Pakistani to reach the double of 1,000 runs and 100 wickets in Test cricket. In 1972, he captained his country to their first overseas tour victory in New Zealand and, on the second tour to England as skipper, his Pakistan side became the first unbeaten touring side since the 1948 Australians. His highest Test score, a violent 138, was made against England, and few will forget his memorable ninth wicket stand of 190 made with Asif at The Oval in 1967.

Jim Laker remembered him as one of the game's true gentlemen, who wore the Surrey cap with great pride and pleasure, and was grateful to count him as a great friend.

R.D. Jackman
RHB & RFMB, 1966-1982

Birth: Simla, India 13/08/1945

Matches: 338 *261*

Batting career for Surrey:

I	NO	HS	Runs
386	132	92*	4823
161	*51*	*46*	*1387*
Av	100s	1000s	
18.98	-	-	
12.60	*-*		

Bowling career for Surrey:

Balls	Runs	Wkts	Av
57342	26969	1206	22.36
12991	*8273*	*399*	*20.73*
Best	5wI	10wM	
8-58	61	7	
7-33	*17*		

Catches: 152 *43*

Tests: 4, 1980/81-1982
ODIs: 15, 1974-1982/83

Robin Jackman first joined Surrey in 1964. He was born in India, his father Ray being a very popular Gurkha officer. The family moved to Guildford when Robin was two, then bought a farm at Bisley, where Robin lived until he left for South Africa for good in 1983. He went to St Edmunds School, Canterbury, where he headed both the batting and bowling averages with the best aggregates in the school's long history.

A short man for a faster bowler, Jackman had a long run up, a good delivery and strong follow-through. He moved the ball both in the air and off the seam and was an effective wicket-taker. His first county game was against Middlesex in 1966 and at the end of that season he decided to further his career by wintering in South Africa. Here started a love affair with the country that would eventually lead to Robin and his South African wife Vonnie setting up home there. He was awarded his county cap in 1970 as his bowling became ever more penetrative and his trademark raucous appeal ever louder. Pat Pocock remembers 'Technically, he was a very fine performer. He was a very aggressive competitor and his best ball was definitely the one that nipped back.'

For Surrey, he was the leading bowler over several years in both first-class and one-day cricket, as borne out by his figures. He also made several useful batting performances throughout

long summer days. Eventually he played for England too. His cricketing excellence earned him his first international call-up in 1974, when he played two one-day internationals against India. However, despite consistently good performances in the county game, he was overlooked on numerous occasions for Test recognition. When Willis was injured early on during the 1980/81 tour to the West Indies, there was complete unanimity in the team about who should be sent as replacement. His South African connections meant the Guyanese government would not let him stay in the country and so the whole England side left, throwing the tour into doubt. After lengthy high-level talks, the trip went ahead and Jackman made his debut at the age of 35 in Barbados. Jackman retired in March 1983, having taken 1,402 first-class wickets at 22.80, including three hat-tricks. With his whole-hearted and thoughtful nature and the respect his character earned him over the years, Jackman did not find it too difficult to forge an equally successful career for himself in cricket commentary in South Africa.

Birth: Malabar Hill, Bombay, India 23/10/1900
Death: Montreux, Switzerland 18/06/1958

Matches: 141

Batting career for Surrey:

I	NO	HS	Runs
194	36	167	7037
Av	100s	1000s	
44.53	14	3	

Bowling career for Surrey:

Balls	Runs	Wkts	Av	Best	5wl
1515	916	25	36.64	2-13	-

Catches: 102

Tests: 22, 1928-1933/34

Douglas Jardine was born in Bombay, India, where his father, M.R. Jardine, spent most of his working life and rose to become Advocate-General of Bombay. He had played first-class cricket for Oxford University, Middlesex and the Europeans. Douglas was initially coached by his father before coming to England to be educated at Winchester, where H.S. Altham and E.R. Wilson coached him. He had a school batting average over 50. He went to Oxford University, winning a Blue in 1920, 1921 and 1923, missing out only because of a knee injury in 1922. He scarcely progressed as expected, but was good enough to attract the interest of Surrey, having qualified by residence.

Fully 6ft tall, he was a good batsman with great power of wrist and forearm. He did not have all the strokes, but showed unusual defensive skill with an unorthodox stance, standing side-on with the bat well away from him. He was at his best in a crisis and had plenty of courage. Integrity, self-belief, obedience and discipline were high on his personal agenda and he expected unquestioning loyalty from any team of which he had charge. He brooked no opposition and asked nothing of a colleague that he would not ask of himself.

He steadily improved and by 1927, despite business commitments, he was the most reliable of amateur batsmen. He hit 1,000 runs in a season eight times, plus once overseas. His highest

aggregate was 1,473, average 46.03, in 1926, but his best seasons were 1927 and 1928, when he headed the first-class averages with figures of 91.09 and 87.15 respectively. His only double century was 214 for MCC *v.* Tasmania at Launceston in 1928/29.

He missed all of 1929 and played fewer matches in 1930 and 1931 due to business pressures. He first captained Surrey in 1932, having been named captain for the 1932/33 Australian tour, causing Percy Fender to step down from the captaincy, much to the disappointment of the Surrey players. To his credit, Fender continued to play and gave his advice on the numerous occasions on which Jardine wanted guidance.

On the 1932/33 tour to Australia, Jardine employed the controversial leg-theory bowling tactics in conjunction with Larwood and Voce. His captaincy caused much ill feeling between England and Australia but he proved successful, winning the series by four matches to one. His 1933 season was curtailed by a long-term injury to his knee. After taking the 1933/34 MCC team to India, Jardine retired from first-class cricket, although still at the height of his powers. He led England in 15 Tests in all, losing only once.

He wrote a book on the 1932/33 tour, *In Quest of the Ashes*, together with various other articles and commentaries on the game.

D.L.A. Jephson ────────────────────────────

RHB & RFB (Under-arm lobs), 1894-1904

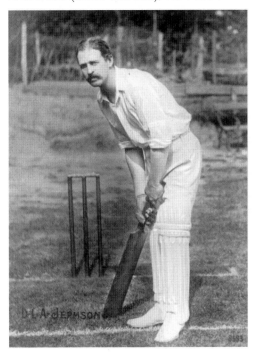

D.L.A. JEPHSON

Birth: Brixton, London 23/02/1871
Death: Cambridge 19/01/1926

Matches: 165

Batting career for Surrey:

I	NO	HS	Runs
237	32	213	6566
Av	100s	1000s	
32.02	9	2	

Bowling career for Surrey:

Balls	Runs	Wkts	Av
11328	5747	249	23.08
Best	5wI	10wM	
7-51	10	1	

Catches: 82

Digby Jephson was a most useful all-round cricketer, fit, when at the height of his powers, for inclusion in any team except those of an international character. He learned the game at Manor House School, Clapham, and developed his skill at Cambridge.

He had the misfortune to be born with one leg shorter than the other. He was of medium height, having distinctive features. His dark hair was centrally parted; his full moustache drooped slightly at the edges. A high brow and Roman nose gave him a scholarly look. As a batsman, he possessed many strokes and could hit very hard indeed, while in the field, he always worked hard. He will, however, always be best remembered for his lob bowling, a style he cultivated after employing fast over-arm for some years. In 1890, he obtained his Blue for Cambridge, but in his three matches against Oxford he scored only 31 runs in three completed innings.

It was for Surrey that most of his greatest feats in first-class cricket were performed. He assisted the county from 1891 until 1904 and in two seasons, 1901 and 1902, captained the side. His highest of the nine three-figure innings he played for Surrey was 213, against

Derbyshire at The Oval in 1900 when he and Abel (193), going in against 325, made 364 together for the first wicket. In the match with Sussex at Hove a year later, the same pair twice made over a hundred together for the opening partnership, 114 in the first innings and 109 in the second. Another large partnership was with Bobby Abel against Gloucestershire at The Oval in 1898 when they added 256 without being parted.

In 1900, he had an excellent all-round record, for, besides making 1,952 runs with an average of 41.53, he took 66 wickets for 23.40 runs each. In the Gentlemen v. Players match at Lord's in 1899, his lobs gained him an analysis of six for 21, a splendid performance against a strong batting side. For Surrey he took five wickets for 12 runs against Derbyshire at Chesterfield in 1899, and performed the hat-trick v. Middlesex at The Oval in 1904.

In club cricket he did many remarkable things, especially for the Wanderers, including two triple-centuries and other large innings over 200 when he also played for Crystal Palace. For some time he was on the London Stock Exchange, but later he took to journalism and coaching on the Cambridge University Cricket Ground. He was the author of a book of verse entitled *A Few Overs*.

RHB, RF(RO)B & WK, 1862-1881

Birth: Dorking, Surrey 19/11/1841
Death: Bermondsey, London 08/04/1889

Matches: 252

Batting career for Surrey:

I	NO	HS	Runs
467	40	165	11452
Av	100s	1000s	
26.81	12	0	

Bowling career for Surrey:

Balls	Runs	Wkts	Av	Best	5wl
635	316	7	45.14	3-75	-

Catches: 148
Stumpings: 6

Tests: 2, 1876/77

Known as 'Harry', he was one of five Jupps to play first-class cricket. Three were not related but his cousin, William Thomas, played two matches for Surrey in 1876. Harry, who was only 5ft 6in tall, was described in his time as one of the best all-round men of his own or any age, an excellent opening bat, an occasional right-arm bowler, a good deep field and an efficient wicketkeeper. His bowling on very rare occasions was only for Surrey, taking just seven wickets.

Jupp grew up in the Dorking area of Surrey where an amalgam of clubs formed a 'Brockham XI' and, with a little poaching, formed a strong team. Harry Jupp was recruited at eighteen years old and was spotted by Surrey when playing against Epsom. In 1861, he was engaged at The Oval, partly as a bricklayer, that being his trade, and partly as a cricketer to the Kennington Club, then a very strong club and the only club who had leave to play at The Oval. In 1863, he became a regular member of the team, and he and his friend Tom Humphrey became notorious as 'the two Surrey boys'. They generally opened the batting and formed the first of the great Surrey opening partnerships.

He was a most prolific batsman with great defensive powers earning him the nickname of 'Young Stonewall'. His best season was 1874 when he scored 1,275 runs, average 36.42, and

against Yorkshire became the first Surrey man to carry his bat in both innings, scoring 43* out of 95 and 109* out of 193. In 1881, he took his benefit at The Oval, which was very profitable. Jupp was a reserved man and those who did not know him thought he was somewhat sulky, which was far from the truth.

He toured with Willsher to North America in 1868 (not first-class) and with Grace to Australia (also not first-class). Going to Australia in 1876/77, he had the distinction of being the first Englishmen to receive a ball in Test cricket and was top scorer for England with 63 in a match lost by 45 runs. It was only recognised as the first Test match at a later date. In the second match, he took over as wicketkeeper from J. Selby after lunch on the first day. He played thirty times in the Gentlemen and Players matches at Lord's and The Oval.

For Surrey, he was responsible for introducing W.W. Read to the club. After retiring, he kept the Sun, the taphouse to the brewery at Dorking, and later kept the Sun Hotel at Weston, near Southampton, after his second marriage. He had to leave owing to his wife's health and was one of the Surrey County umpires from 1883 to 1888.

Birth: Streatham, London 11/101/1864
Death: Wittersham, Kent 09/08/1932

Matches: 288

Batting career for Surrey:

I	NO	HS	Runs
423	55	179	9654
Av	100s	1000s	
26.23	8	1	

Bowling career for Surrey:

Balls	Runs	Wkts	Av	Best	5wI
440	195	5	39.00	2-36	-

Catches: 80

Sir Kingsmill James Key succeeded John Shuter as captain of Surrey in 1894 and stayed in the role for six seasons, during which Surrey were County Champions in 1894, 1895 and 1899. He first made his name with a notable performance in company with W.E. Roller. First playing for Surrey in 1882, at the age of seventeen, he had accomplished nothing of special note until he and Roller found themselves, in August 1883, playing against Lancashire – Surrey were set 234 to win and by late on the second afternoon they had lost seven wickets for 122 and looked doomed to defeat. At that point, Key joined Roller and, so ably did these two young men bat that before the drawing of stumps, 56 runs had been obtained without further loss. Next morning, Key (60) and Roller (55) hit off the remaining runs and so not only gained victory for Surrey, but established their individual reputations. Key, in later years, had many fine batting performances, but nothing was more remarkable than this memorable display at the age of eighteen.

Educated at Clifton, Key not only showed great promise as a batsman but also as a slow bowler. In his last year at school against Cheltenham, he scored 90 and 1 and took five wickets. Against Sherborne, he scored 59 and took 5 wickets for 31. At Oxford, he obtained his Blue as a fresher and played Cambridge on four occasions. In 1886, his greatest triumph in the University match was an innings of 143 when he and W.W. Rashleigh put on 243 for the first wicket. Another memorable performance was his partnership with H. Philipson against Middlesex at Chiswick Park in 1887, Key made 281 and Philipson 150, the partnership of 340 being at the time the largest on record in first-class cricket.

Key's connection as an active player with Surrey lasted 17 years and during this period he scored 12,928 runs in all first-class matches. He appeared for Gentlemen against Players between 1885 and 1889, and went to America with E.J. Sanders's team in 1886 and Lord Hawke's team in 1891.

A fine, free, powerful batsman, Key also possessed a very strong defence and had at his command all sorts of strokes. He played back with a dead straight bat and could force the ball away with great power. He was never more in his element than in times of difficulty. Indeed, a position of anxiety or disaster brought out his highest skill. Finally, he was a man of most original views, a philosophical cricketer and an imperturbable captain.

He also attained some excellence as a rugby football player and appeared in the Varsity match in 1885 and in 1886.

Birth: Sutton, Surrey 12/05/1894
Death: Marylebone, London 05/01/1960

Matches: 107

Batting career for Surrey:

I	NO	HS	Runs
159	11	146	4390
Av	100s	1000s	
29.66	9	0	

Bowling career for Surrey:

Balls	Runs	Wkts	Av	Best	5wl
24	2	3	0.66	2-0	-

Catches: 52

Tests: 2, 1921

There are some gifted cricketers who from early boyhood seem marked out for distinction. It is to this select band that Donald John Knight unquestionably belongs. He was a born batsman, very good to look at, always easy and graceful in style specially strong on the on-side and also a master of a beautiful late cut. He was tried with no great success as a slip fielder, but his true vocation was at deep third man and in the long field.

In five seasons in the Malvern XI from 1909 to 1913, two of them spent as captain, he displayed such ability that he hit 2,860 runs at an average of almost 47. During his schooldays he appeared for the Surrey Second XI when barely fifteen, scoring 53 and making his first-class debut two years later. At Oxford, he gained his Blue as a fresher in 1914 and following the First World War, in which he served with the 28th London Regiment (Artists), he made 35 and 78 in the Varsity match in 1919, being on the winning side on each occasion.

In the latter season he enjoyed special success, sharing in a number of splendid opening stands for Surrey with Jack Hobbs and scoring altogether 1,588 runs at 45.37. His nine centuries included 114 and 101 in the match with Yorkshire at The Oval and he obtained 71 and 124 for Gentlemen against Players at Lord's.

He became a schoolmaster at Westminster in 1920 in which season he received a heavy blow on the head when fielding at short-leg and never again recovered his old form. He played some eleven matches for the county in 1920, producing a highest score of 52. He played in two Test matches for England against Warwick Armstrong's Australians in 1921. Thenceforward, he could spare little time for cricket, but he managed a few games in 1923 when he was his old self, having recovered his confidence, averaging 53.00 in seven innings. In 1937, at the age of 43, he was persuaded to take part in twelve matches for Surrey, scoring 584 runs, including 105 against Hampshire at The Oval, average 24.33. However, artist with the bat that he still was, he could no longer stand the strain of long days in the field and he quietly dropped out of the side.

In lesser cricket, he performed well for Oxford Harlequins, Old Malvernians and Sutton and holds the record for the highest score on the present Wimbledon ground when scoring 205* for Sutton in 1926. The ease and elegance of his batting made him one of the great stylists of the game. He was a generous and modest man who was as graceful and noble off the field as he was on it.

R.D.V. Knight
LHB & RMB, 1968-1984

Birth: Streatham, London 06/09/1946

Matches: 174 *160*

Batting career for Surrey:

I	NO	HS	Runs
290	32	142	8712
148	*15*	*92**	*3116*
Av	100s	1000s	
33.76	15	6	
23.42	*0*		

Bowling career for Surrey:

Balls	Runs	Wkts	Av	Best	5wI
12257	5549	163	34.04	5-44	2
5856	*3889*	*147*	*26.45*	*4-19*	*2*

Catches: 137 *44*

Roger Knight was invited to rejoin Surrey as their captain in 1978, was capped and led the side for six seasons during which they won the NatWest Trophy in 1982. In his first season as captain, Surrey finished 16th in the County Championship and tenth in the Sunday League. However, there was great improvement in the following years when they finished third in 1979, second in 1980, sixth in 1981, fifth in 1982 and eighth in 1983. He scored 6,797 runs during these years and he said about this period 'To be invited to return to The Oval as captain was a challenge not to be missed. Instead of being a schoolmaster who played county cricket, I needed to become a county cricket captain who taught in the winter. The years of my captaincy were a very stimulating period and an opportunity to work with some very talented cricketers.' Awarded a benefit in 1984, Roger Knight retired from first-class cricket at the end of that season to return to full-time teaching.

Roger was educated at Dulwich School (playing in the First XI for four years) and went to Cambridge University from 1967 to 1970, gaining his Blue in all four years. Meanwhile, he played for Surrey Young Cricketers and Surrey Second XI, making his first-class debut in 1968.

In 1970, Surrey had a very talented side and as Roger Knight could not find a first team

place, he moved to Gloucestershire, for whom he played 105 first-class matches. At the end of 1974, he moved to Sussex, where he taught at Eastbourne College and played 43 first-class matches for them in 1976 and 1977. Capped by all three counties for whom he played, he had the unique distinction of scoring more than 1,000 runs for each county in the John Player League.

He must be considered extremely unlucky never to have been selected for an England tour, let alone actually play for England. With an honest and open approach to the game of cricket and the model way in which he conducted himself both on and off the field, his peers held him in high esteem. His tours included D.H. Robin's XI to South Africa 1972/73, MCC to East Africa 1973/74, MCC to West Africa 1975/76 (not first-class) and an Overseas XI to India 1980/81.

He played some Minor Counties cricket for Bedfordshire in 1987 and 1988. In his first-class career, he played 387 matches, scoring 19,558 runs (average 32. 00) with 31 centuries and took 369 wickets (average 36.13).

In 1984, Roger Knight took up full-time teaching as housemaster at Cranleigh School and, from 1990 to 1993, was headmaster at Workshop College. In 1994, he was appointed secretary and chief executive of MCC, a position he still holds.

Birth: Clapham, London 10/10/1884
Death: Surbiton, Surrey 03/03/1935

Matches: 73

Batting career for Surrey:

I	NO	HS	Runs
106	30	27*	670
Av	100s	1000s	
8.81	-	-	

Bowling career for Surrey:

Balls	Runs	Wkts	Av
12384	7269	347	20.94
Best	5wI	10wM	
8-48	31	8	

Catches: 27

Tests: 2, 1907

The cricket career of Neville Knox was brief but brilliant. In his formative years, he played both cricket and rugby football for Dulwich College, and he first appeared for Surrey against Lancashire in 1904, when he took four wickets. The following season, he rose to fame in remarkable fashion and had a big share in winning for Surrey a high position among the counties, after a year of extreme depression. For the county he took 121 wickets and in all matches dismissed 129 batsmen at an average of less than 22 runs apiece.

In the following year he did even better, taking 144 wickets for 19.63 runs each and achieving a notable triumph for the Gentlemen against the Players at Lord's by taking 12 wickets for 183. He had a large share in a victory for the Gentlemen by 45 runs, seven of his victims being clean bowled. It was astonishing how H. Martyn, the Oxford and Somerset wicketkeeper, stood up to his tremendously fast bowling. In the same game, Arthur Fielder, the Kent fast bowler, performed the feat, never previously accomplished in this fixture, of taking, at a cost of 90 runs, all ten wickets in the Gentlemen's first innings.

The first-class career of Knox ended in 1910. He developed an acute form of shin soreness and had to struggle against chronic lameness. He often played when he ought to have been resting and only sheer pluck and resolution enabled him to get through the work he did. Loose-limbed and standing well over 6ft, Knox made full use of his physical advantage. His long and peculiar run, starting from near deep mid-off, made the length and direction of the ball difficult to judge. He bowled at a great pace with an undeniable off-break, and his good-length deliveries often reared up straight.

In 1907, he played for England against South Africa in the second and third Test matches at Headingley and Kennington Oval without, however, achieving much success. In *Wisden Cricketers Almanack*, Hobbs, referring to fast bowlers, said: 'Being a member of the same county side, I only played against N.A. Knox in Gentlemen and Players matches and games of a similar description, when he was probably past his best, but I think he was the best fast bowler I ever saw.' He was rated by some as very nearly as fine a bowler as Lockwood or Richardson.

During the First World War, Knox joined the RAOC as a lieutenant in 1915 and was promoted to captain in 1919.

Birth: Frizinghall, Yorkshire 09/02/1922
Death: Putney, London 23/04/1986

Matches: 309

Batting career for Surrey:

I	NO	HS	Runs
387	70	113	5531
Av	100s	1000s	
17.44	2	-	

Bowling career for Surrey:

Balls	Runs	Wkts	Av
69653	24236	1395	17.37
Best	5wI	10wM	
10-88	93	24	

Catches: 223

Tests: 46, 1947/48-1958/59

Jim Laker is known in cricket history as the bowler to take 19 wickets in the Old Trafford Test match against the Australians in 1956. He actually took all ten wickets against the Aussies on two occasions in that year, and achieved the outstanding figures of 8 for 2 in the Bradford Test trial of 1950. It is odd that his genius did not emerge in the pre-war nets at Headingley. Attending Saltaire School, Jim was a batsman and fast bowler and, at fifteen, he played for his school in the mornings and Saltaire in the Bradford league in the afternoons. At sixteen, he attended the indoor cricket school at Headingley.

The war came, and before he joined the army in 1941, Jim spent two years working for Barclays Bank in Bradford. Posted to North Africa, he began to play some limited cricket after El Alamein in Cairo where, on matting, he was able to spin the ball as he had never spun it before. Peter Smith did his best to persuade Jim to join Essex and he might well have done so if he had not pulled out of a trial because of a raw spinning finger. Ironically, Jim ended his career with Essex when he left Surrey after a disagreement with the Surrey Committee over comments in his book *Over to Me*.

Back in England awaiting his demobilisation, he was billeted with a friend at Catford. Jim joined the local cricket club, whose president, Andrew Kempton, introduced him to Surrey. Errol Holmes needed no second thoughts at Jim's trial in the nets and Yorkshire, blissfully unaware of the treasure they were passing over, readily consented to his registration.

After one match in 1946, against Combined Services, 1947 saw his Championship debut. Success was instant, top of Surrey averages and seventh in the national listings. He was selected for the tour to the West Indies and in his first Test at Barbados, he took 7 for 103 in the second innings, including 6 for 25 in his last nine overs. Laker earned fulsome praise, but in his heart he knew he could have bowled better.

Laker was always a thoughtful and intelligent cricketer, and his native common sense helped him over the bad times. The English Test selectors nonetheless showed little faith in him during the next eight years and he was never sure of his place in the England side.

He was not chosen for the 1950/51 or the 1954/55 tours of Australia, although he did go to the West Indies in 1953/54. It was a widely held belief that an off-spinner was a passenger on Australian pitches until Laker, despite an arthritic finger, took 15 of the 45 wickets to fall

in the four matches in which he played in 1958/59 and headed the averages. After the 1953 and 1956 series in England, the Australians complained that the pitches were doctored for Lock and Laker. The revenge, complete and ruthless, was to be taken at home. Sure enough, the surfaces gave Laker no help, but not once were the Aussies able to carry out their threats. He proved he was the absolute master of control, accuracy, flight and guile; the technical perfectionist.

The Laker legend of 1956 began in mid-May when he took 10 wickets in an innings for Surrey as they beat the Australians by ten wickets to become the first county to defeat an Australian team in 44 years. During his 13 seasons with Surrey, the title was won a record seven times in successive years, and was shared once. It is highly improbable The Oval will see his like again, or a combination to match Lock and Laker. His figures speak for themselves and his contribution to the Championship-winning sequence was immense. Jim Laker took three hat-tricks for Surrey – against Gloucestershire at Gloucester in 1951 and twice in 1953, against Warwickshire at The Oval and Cambridge University at Guildford. He made useful runs as a lower-order batsman, twice scoring centuries, 100 v. Cambridge University at Guildford in 1949 and 113 against Gloucestershire at The Oval in 1954. In the Guildford match, he shared in a record eighth-wicket partnership of 173 with Bernie Constable.

With his commanding height, high action, hands large enough to make the ball positively hum through the air, and the mental and physical strength to bowl with unswerving accuracy for long stretches, Laker was the ultimate off-spinner, a model for every student at any level of the game. Unassuming, quiet and undemonstrative, but knowing his own mind, Jim became a respected television commentator and, as befits a consummate artist and professional, his knowledge came shining through.

Birth: Sowerby Bridge, Yorkshire 25/12/1875
Death: West Hartlepool, Co. Durham 10/09/1924

Matches: 343

Batting career for Surrey:

I	NO	HS	Runs
48	68	137	7237
Av	100s	1000s	
17.23	2	0	

Bowling career for Surrey:

Balls	Runs	Wkts	Av
66037	28542	1331	21.44
Best	5wI	10wM	
9-81	92	20	

Catches: 118

Tests: 5, 1905/06

Though perhaps never in quite the front rank of bowlers, being very good without being great, Walter Lees had a long and distinguished career. A Yorkshireman, he won nearly all his fame for Surrey, playing his first match for the county in 1896 and staying on until 1911. He played his early cricket in Halifax, but joined Surrey after answering an advertisement by Surrey CCC to become a member of the groundstaff.

His best days were from 1903 to 1910. In those eight seasons, he took 1,031 wickets for 20.5 runs each in first-class matches in England. He was particularly successful in 1905, when 193 wickets fell to him. Always on the quick side of medium pace, he was very accurate and with a good delivery made the ball come off the pitch with plenty of life. Some peculiarity in the flight of the ball rather than his break made it difficult to read. Hard wickets suited him much better than soft ones.

He was picked for Players against Gentlemen at The Oval in 1904, at Lord's in 1905 and at both grounds in 1906. Lees did particularly well in the 1906 match at Lord's when he took six wickets. Incidentally, in getting 51 on the last day, he faced Knox and Brearley with far more confidence than any of the Players except Hayward and Hayes. He was more than a useful batsman, twice hitting up a hundred for Surrey, 130 against Hampshire at Aldershot in 1905 and 137 against Sussex at The Oval in 1906.

He was never picked for a tour in Australia, but he went with the MCC team to South Africa in 1905/06. It was a disastrous tour, the Englishmen being baffled by leg-break spin bowling on matting wickets from Vogler, Schwarz, Faulkner and White. They won only one Test match and lost the other four, although Lees took 26 wickets at 12.96 in the series.

Lees had his benefit at The Oval in 1906 and profited to the extent of £1,356. Over these three days, 66,923 sixpences were taken at the gates. Lees' best performances as a bowler were a hat-trick against Hampshire at Southampton in 1897, and bowling unchanged with Rushby through both innings against Lancashire at Old Trafford in 1898. Against London County at The Oval in 1904, he took five wickets for seven runs in 42 balls, his victims including W.G. Grace, W.L. Murdoch, A.C. MacLaren and L.O.S Poidevin. The same season, he took 5 for 7 runs in 55 balls *v.* Hampshire on the same ground. His best bowling performance was 9 for 81 against Sussex at Eastbourne in 1905.

H.D.G. Leveson-Gower
RHB & RLBB, 1895-1920

Birth: Titsey Place, Surrey 08/05/1873
Death: Kensington, London 01/02/1954

Matches: 122

Batting career for Surrey:

I	NO	HS	Runs
174	27	155	3308
Av	100s	1000s	
22.50	2	-	

Bowling career for Surrey:

Balls	Runs	Wkts	Av	Best	5wl
345	211	2	105.50	1-12	-

Catches: 38

Tests: 3, 1909/10

Sir Henry Dudley Gresham Leveson-Gower was known as 'Shrimp' wherever he played cricket, a nickname given to him in his schooldays, presumably because of his slight physique. He was born the seventh of twelve sons of Mr G.W.G. Leveson-Gower. At Winchester School, he was one of three brothers to gain colours at cricket where, according to him, he really learned the game. He led the school to their first victory at Eton for ten years.

At Magdalen College, Oxford, he got his Blue as a fresher in 1893, and figured in the team in the following three years, being captain in 1896. Against Cambridge, he scored 73 in 1895 and took 7 wickets for 84 runs. That season he began his association with Surrey that continued until his death. A skilful right-handed batsman and a keen fielder, usually at cover-point or mid-off, he hit his highest innings, 155, against his former university at Oxford in 1899. He captained Surrey from 1908 to 1910.

Standing only 5ft 8in tall, he used a light bat and was a good off-side player. He was an admirable captain who knew the game well, always giving the impression of being happy and cheerful. A great man in a crisis, he inspired others with his courage and determination, and at cover-point, he was a keen and active fielder.

On several occasions, he appeared for Gentlemen against Players. From 1899 until

1950, he was responsible for the selection of the sides taking part in the Scarborough Festival. Leveson-Gower also had considerable experience of cricket outside England. He went to South Africa with MCC teams in 1905/06 and 1909/10, being captain on the second occasion. He visited the West Indies under Lord Hawke in 1896/97 and, in the autumn of 1897, toured America with the side captained by P.F. Warner. Between 1928 and 1934, he also played with teams in Malta, Gibraltar and Portugal. Altogether in first-class cricket, he scored 7,662 runs, average 22.88.

Aside from his playing ability, probably his greatest service to cricket, for which he was knighted in 1953, was rendered as a legislator and Test selector. For many years a member of the MCC Committee, he was Surrey treasurer from 1926 to 1928 and president of the County Club for twenty years from 1929. He remained on the committee for the rest of his life.

During the First World War, he served in the Army, attaining the rank of major and being mentioned in dispatches. He contributed articles to *Wisden* in 1937 on 'Recollections of Oxford Cricket' and, in 1946, on '100 Years of Surrey Cricket'. He also wrote the book *On and Off the Field*.

P.J. Loader

RHB & RFB, 1951-1963

Birth: Wallington, Surrey 25/10/1929

Matches: 298 /

Batting career for Surrey:

I	NO	HS	Runs
291	87	81	1827
/	0	/	/
Av	**100s**	**1000s**	
8-95	-	-	
1.00	-		

Bowling career for Surrey:

Balls	Runs	Wkts	Av
50919	20685	1108	18.66
90	25	3	11.66
Best	**5wl**	**10wM**	
9-17	65	13	
3-35			

Catches: 99 0

Tests: 13, 1954-1958/59

In 1957, Peter Loader earned fame by performing the hat-trick in the Fourth Test match with the West Indies, a feat never previously accomplished by an England player in a home Test. In seven successive years, he made a great contribution to help Surrey to win the County Championship. His pace, his ability to make the ball 'move' late in its flight and his skill in disguising the occasional slower delivery placed him in the forefront of fast bowlers.

Born in Wallington, Surrey, Loader felt the irresistible urge for speed in his bowling from the age of seven and, although he received no coaching, he developed sufficient skill to play for Beddington CC by the age of fifteen. A game against Surrey Club and Ground in 1950 was followed by an invitation to assist the Club and Ground team. The next year he had the chance to play for the first team against Kent, but took only three wickets for 96 runs in two innings. Coaching by Andrew Sandham, and help from Alec Bedser, brought a steady improvement in the young bowler. Given a contract in 1952, he played in six matches, taking 28 wickets at 22.07.

In 1953, his tally of wickets shot up to 80 at 18.28 runs each and, between July 8 and 17, in three matches he took 34 wickets, average 7.97. A visit with the Commonwealth team to India

helped to build up Loader's somewhat slight physique, and in 1954 he disposed of 109 batsmen, average 14.57. That season he came to notice by taking 7 wickets for 37 in the Gentlemen's first innings at Lord's, gaining him selection for England in the last Test match with Pakistan. The next winter he went to Australia, but with Statham and Tyson, the other fast bowlers, in such devastating form, he was not chosen for a Test. He took 41 wickets at less than 20 runs apiece in other matches. In 1955, he secured 96 wickets, average 17.65 and in 1956, he took 124 wickets at 15.69.

For England in South Africa the next winter, Loader took only nine wickets in four Test matches, but in 1957 he had his best season with 133 first-class wickets at 15.47, including 6 for 36 in the first West Indies innings of the Headingley Test. He toured Australia again in 1958/59, and it was only because England had a cache of fast bowlers that he received so few chances in Test cricket.

Besides his bowling, he was a keen, safe fielder in the deep. On leaving Surrey in 1963, he emigrated to Western Australia, where he is now a businessman and cricket broadcaster.

Birth: Limpsfield, Surrey 05/07/1929
Death: Perth, Australia 29/03/1995

Matches: 385

Batting career for Surrey:

I	NO	HS	Runs
451	100	70	5391
Av	100s	1000s	
15.35	-	-	

Bowling career for Surrey:

Balls	Runs	Wkts	Av
83270	29835	1713	17.41
Best	5wI	10wM	
10-54	123	31	

Catches: 533

Tests: 49, 1952-1967/68

Tony Lock played as a boy for the Limpsfield and Oxted clubs, as well as the Surrey Colts. In 1946, he was offered a contract by Surrey and made his first-class debut eight days after his seventeenth birthday to became the youngest ever Surrey player, a record that still stands. After a period of National Service, during which he played two first-class matches for the Combined Services, he became a regular member of the county side in 1949.

Although his slow left-arm bowling was successful, it was clear that, to make further progress, he needed to spin the ball more. It is said that in the winter of 1951/52, he was coaching at a South London cricket school where the roof was so low that he had to lower his arm and quicken his pace through the air, rather than use flight, and this enabled him to increase the amount of spin. In 1952, especially on pitches that gave him any assistance, he became almost a medium-paced bowler, but doubts were raised as to the legitimacy of his action. Almost immediately after his first Test appearance for England in 1952, he was no-balled three times – twice in an over, for throwing in the county match against the Indian touring side. In 1954, he was again no-balled by three umpires during the winter tour of the West Indies. After the 1958/59 tour to

Australia and New Zealand, he saw a slow-motion film of his action.

Approaching his thirtieth birthday, he probably felt that he had another ten years of first-class cricket in him, but was quite shocked after watching himself on film. In addition, Australia, where he had taken only five wickets in four Test matches, proved that on a hard fast pitch, his faster trajectory would never be beneficial to him. Within a matter of weeks, he became yet another bowler. The jerks and kinks had been removed from his action, which was now faultless. Even so, he was no-balled in 1959 and in 1960, although by 1961, the England selectors were sufficiently satisfied with his action that he was back in the Test team.

Sadly, Surrey saw very little of the new Tony Lock. He was not only disappointed with the outcome of his benefit, but also thoroughly disenchanted at being omitted from the MCC tour to Australia in 1962/63. That winter, he flew out to Perth to fulfil a contract to play for Western Australia and decided almost immediately that this was to be his future home. He returned to play his final season for Surrey in 1963, after which he tidied up his affairs and asked his wife, Audrey, and their two sons to join him in Perth.

In early March 1968, England in the West Indies called up Lock when Titmus was badly injured. In the final Test at Georgetown, England remained undefeated in the series, thanks to an eighth-wicket partnership by Lock and Pocock of 109, with Lock scoring 89, his highest score in first-class cricket.

During the seven Championship-winning years in the 1950s, Tony Lock took 817 wickets, and in the 1956 season, in two matches against Kent, he captured 26 wickets for 143, 10 at The Oval and 16 at Blackheath including 10 for 54 in the second innings, his personal best performance.

After the 1963 season, he emigrated to Perth and became a regular member of the Western Australian State team, and was appointed captain in 1967/68. He took 316 wickets for them, and led them to victory in the Sheffield Shield. Whilst living in Australia, he was persuaded to return to England to play for and captain Leicestershire. He had two successful seasons with the county, and his enthusiasm was a factor in the successes that were to follow in the 1970s. In 1971, he retired from first-class cricket and lived the rest of his life in Australia, becoming a naturalised citizen in 1982. He returned to England to coach at Mill Hill School, London, from 1987 to 1991.

Had he never taken a wicket, he would still be remembered as one of the game's greatest fielders close to the bat. Usually fielding at short leg, in the days before fielding helmets had been thought of, he took some outstanding catches, as he also did off his own bowling. He was one of the team of fielders that so intimidated batsmen during the great years of Surridge's captaincy. He will be remembered not just for his performances for the county, but also for the style of his approach to the game.

Birth: Old Radford, Nottinghamshire 25/03/1868
Death: Old Radford, Nottinghamshire 26/04/1932

Matches: 306

Batting career for Surrey:

I	NO	HS	Runs
446	33	165	9299
Av	100s	1000s	
22.51	14	2	

Bowling career for Surrey:

Balls	Runs	Wkts	Av
44143	21266	1182	17.99
Best	5wI	10wM	
9-59	105	27	

Catches: 117

Tests: 12, 1893-1902

In his day as one of the finest fast bowlers the game of cricket has ever known, Lockwood had a somewhat chequered career. Born at Old Radford, Nottinghamshire, he played his early cricket for Forest Wanderers and Nottingham Forest Cricket Association. Lockwood was given a trial for Nottinghamshire in 1886, but accomplished nothing of note, and in the following year he accepted an engagement on the groundstaff at Kennington Oval. He duly qualified for Surrey, and although Notts were anxious to secure his services in 1889, he preferred to stay with his adopted county who outbid Nottinghamshire for his services. In that season, he signalised his association with Surrey with an innings of 83 against Nottinghamshire in the August Bank Holiday match at The Oval. Throughout his career, he played in 24 matches against the county of his birth, scoring 891 runs (average 27. 84) and taking 78 wickets (average 22. 06).

Not until two years later did he make his mark as a bowler, his great performance that summer being 11 wickets for 40 runs against Kent at The Oval. In 1892, when Surrey had George Lohmann and Tom Richardson as well as Lockwood, he headed the averages for all matches, taking 168 wickets for less than 12.5 runs apiece. Lockwood continued to be a great bowler during the next two seasons, but going out to Australia in 1894/95, he failed deplorably and, on his return home, went down hill so rapidly that in 1897 he lost his place in the Surrey team.

Happily, in the ensuing winter, he was at great pains to get himself fit and, in 1898, obtained 134 wickets and scored nearly 1,000 runs in first-class matches. At The Oval, with the ground in excellent condition, he and Tom Richardson dismissed the strong Yorkshire side twice in less than a day for 78 and 186, helping Surrey to win by an innings and 272 runs by the second evening. This must rank as one of the most wonderful exhibitions of fast bowling ever seen, with Lockwood taking 11 for 126 and Richardson 7 for 100. He remained a splendid bowler for several years after this, but finally dropped out of the Surrey team in 1904, having achieved the 'double' in both 1899 and 1900. His best bowling performance for Surrey was 9 for 59 against Essex at Leyton in 1902. For Surrey, he took eight wickets in an innings on 13 occasions.

In 1902, he appeared for England against Australia in four of the five Test matches, and in the contest at Manchester, he secured 11 wickets for 76 runs, so accomplishing one of the greatest bowling performances ever witnessed. To begin with, the pitch proved so soft that it was not until the score reached 129 that Lockwood was given a bowl, but he then dismissed six batsmen for 48, restricting the total to 299. In Australia's second innings, Lockwood got rid of Trumper, Hill and Duff while the score was reaching 10. Lockwood dominated the game, taking 5 wickets for 28, and the tourists were all out for 86. England had to make only 124, but a night's heavy rain placed batsmen at a big disadvantage and Australia, despite Lockwood's magnificent work, won by three runs.

Lockwood did not take such a long run as his famous colleague, Tom Richardson, and he did not appear to be quite so fast through the air. When he was at the top of his form, however, no one ever came off the pitch much faster than he or, with his off-break also a distinguishing quality of his bowling, nor was anyone more difficult to play under conditions favourable to batting. He also had at his command a slow ball, which in his early days he sent down without any perceptible change of delivery. After he 'came back' in 1898, he did not bowl this ball quite as well as before, but it was still a very useful part of his equipment.

In addition to being one of the most famous bowlers of his generation, Lockwood was also a first-rate batsman and had he not been compelled to concentrate his energies upon the taking of wickets, he would, no doubt, have attained high rank as a run-getter. He scored fifteen centuries in his career, his highest score being 165 against Leicestershire at The Oval in 1900. Among his many triumphs was one for the Players against the Gentlemen at Lord's in 1902, when in addition to taking nine wickets for less than 12 runs apiece, he put together an innings of 100.

During his playing career, he took three hat-tricks – the first in 1893 at Fenner's against Cambridge University, the second at The Oval in 1901 against Derbyshire and the third at Sheffield in 1903 against Yorkshire. In all, he played 362 first-class matches, scoring 10,673 runs at an average of 21.96 and taking 1,376 wickets at 18.34 runs each.

Birth: Old Town, Croydon, Surrey 01/11/1826
Death: Croydon, Surrey 22/12/1869

Matches: 124

Batting career for Surrey:

I	NO	HS	Runs
197	31	108*	2588
Av	100s	1000s	
15.59	1	-	

Bowling career for Surrey:

Balls	Runs	Wkts	Av
3535	1742	93	18.73
Best	5wl	10wM	
6-33	9	1	

Catches: 168
Stumpings: 62

Tom was the first 'official' Surrey wicketkeeper, and was regarded as the equal of any wicketkeeper in England around 1860. He held the position from 1849-1866, by which time he was 39. Surprisingly, only 230 (168ct, 62st) of his dismissals were for Surrey in 124 matches. He played a further 99 representative matches, including two tours, the first with Parr to North America 1859 (not first-class) and Australia in 1863/64 (before Test matches).

He was a professional middle-order, right-hand batsman, right-hand fast-medium round-arm bowler and an excellent wicketkeeper, described as stout-hearted. He was 5ft 10in tall, his safe capacious hands were often referred to as 'saucepans'. Tall, brawny and with exceptionally long arms, Tom was one of the first stumpers to take legside deliveries instead of relying on his long-stop. He kept wicket in the transitional period when underarm bowling moved through round-arm to over-arm, with the according variety of bounce. He wore no pads in his early days, but he wore gloves and pads long before the end of his career.

Most of his bowling was for Surrey for whom he took five wickets in an innings nine times, including 5 for 37 against Nottinghamshire at Trent Bridge and, on one occassion, ten in a match. In batting his top score was 108*, his only century, against Nottinghamshire at The

Oval in July 1864. His batting was often of decisive value in Surrey matches, as well as contests between North and South. In 1861, along with W. Caffyn, he made the record stand of 112 for the eighth wicket, the highest by any team against the North.

Though usually a good-natured man, he was considered to be a little 'queer-tempered' on occasions because he liked to get away from the field of play. He showed a preference for his own company at lunch intervals, going off on his own to enjoy a quiet meal and smoke a reflective pipe. In those days, before the invention of cricket sweaters, Tom was instantly recognisable for the white flannel jacket he always wore to keep out the cold; he wore a shorter version on warmer days. He had an extensive knowledge of the game and its laws and was a sublime exponent of the arts of gamesmanship. In his first-class career, he scored 4,917 runs at 15.86, took 119 wickets at 20.06, took 301 catches and made 123 stumpings.

When the younger and talented Pooley came along, he foresaw retirement and became a successful 'Mine Host' of the Prince Albert Inn and the Sheldon Arms in his native Croydon. His physical well-being deteriorated quickly after his playing days ended and he died in his chair at the Sheldon Arms of consumption, shortly before Christmas Day in 1869, aged only forty-three.

Birth: Kensington, London 02/06/1865
Death: Cape Province, S. Africa 01/12/1901

Matches: 186

Batting career for Surrey:

I	NO	HS	Runs
269	25	115	5070
Av	100s	1000s	
20.77	2	-	

Bowling career for Surrey:

Balls	Runs	Wkts	Av
45741	16108	1221	13.19
Best	5wI	10wM	
9-67	128	41	

Catches: 203

Tests: 18, 1886-1896

Owing to ill health (he died in South Africa of tuberculosis when he was only thirty-six) George Lohmann had a sadly short career, albeit a glorious one. His rise was meteoric. Within two seasons of joining the Surrey staff in 1884, he was taking 12 Australian wickets in a Test match on his home ground and spearheading an English victory.

His cricket was learned on Wandsworth Common, early matches being with Church Institute in 1876. He was a completely natural cricketer with a superb physique. Standing 5ft 11in and weighing 12st 12lb, he was broad-shouldered and very good-looking, with fair hair and a moustache, attractive blue eyes set rather wide apart, a bright colour and a fine figure. Although he was no more than medium-fast, he had a repertoire that kept the batsmen guessing. 'Owing to his naturally high delivery the ball described a pronounced curve and dropped rather sooner than the batsman expected. He was the perfect master of the whole art of varying his pace,' wrote C.B. Fry. Lohmann had spin and cut, as well as flight, and the heart to bowl all day.

In only 186 matches for Surrey, he took 1,458 wickets, a striking rate of very nearly eight a match. Even for England, his striking rate of 6.2 a match has been bettered only by

S.F. Barnes. In his first three Tests in Australia, all at Sydney in 1886/87, Lohmann took 25 wickets for 189 runs. In the period from 1885 to 1891, he took more wickets, 1,044, than anyone else in the country. Lohmann was equally successful for England in Australia on each of his three tours, and in 1887/88 took 63 wickets in first-class matches at 11.98. On his tour to South Africa in 1895/96, he proved altogether too much for the opposition and produced some startling performances in the Tests, including 9 for 28 at Johannesburg. He played in 20 matches for Players against Gentlemen, scoring 457 runs (average 17. 57) and taking 89 wickets (average 18. 19) in this series. In all first-class cricket, he scored 7,248 runs and took 1,841 wickets.

Moreover, he could bat too, when he put his mind to it. A dashing, hard-hitting batsman, he scored three centuries in his career, and was magnificent in the field – the finest of all the famous slips up to his time.

Owing to ill health, his career was relatively short and, with the financial help of Surrey Club, he emigrated to South Africa in the hope that the climate might benefit him. He played two seasons for Western Province in 1894/95 and 1896/97.

Birth: Cheam, Surrey 18/12/1940

Matches: 352 / 26

Batting career for Surrey:

I	NO	HS	Runs
409	90	92	4999
98	27	71	1065
Av	100s	1000s	
15.67	-	-	
15.00	-		

Catches: 702 / 10
Stumpings: 103 22

Arnold Long went to Wallington Grammar School, where he was spotted by Surrey at a young age. He made his first-class career in 1960 when Roy Swetman was injured. He played in only one first team match in 1961 against Cambridge University but kept wicket regularly for the Second XI. Swetman retired unexpectedly at the end of the season, and Long then played in all 28 Championship matches in 1962, claiming 91 dismissals, 74 catches and 17 stumpings. Unfortunately, he missed several matches in 1963 when suffering from acute appendicitis.

In 1964, he set a world wicketkeeping record by taking 7 catches in an innings and 11 in the match against Sussex at Hove. During the 1965 to 1967 seasons, he continued to keep wicket well, but his batting was very disappointing. He captained the side on occasions when Micky Stewart was not available. In 1968, he had a top score of 68 playing in all matches, and in 1970 made the highest score of his career with 92 in a year when he scored 643 first-class runs. A complete team player, an outstanding 'keeper and a more than useful bat, he was a quiet man and would never appeal unless he was sure the batsman was out. He would have stood a good chance of playing for England had the gloves not been so firmly in the hands of Alan Knott. He had an enviable ability to switch off the minute he left the field, and would be found in a corner immersed in a text-book as soon as the pads were off.

His benefit season was 1971, the year that Surrey won the Championship. In 1972, he played in all matches, but in 1975 Skinner was introduced as wicketkeeper and, as Long was not offered a contract at the end of the season, he left the club.

If Surrey had lost interest, others had not and Sussex snapped him up to become their first 'imported' 'keeper. He played 97 first-class matches for them and in 1978 was made captain and led Sussex to win the Gillette Cup. He retired at the end of the 1980 season, having played 452 first-class matches in which he had a total of 1,046 dismissals (922 caught and 124 stumped). Mainly through the influence of Micky Stewart, he joined the cricket sub-committee at The Oval and was elected to the Surrey general committee in 1990. As a life vice-president, he has actively continued his involvement with the club.

In 1972, he set up in partnership in the insurance business being fully qualified, dealing with general insurance and financial planning. Married to Barbara with three children, the family live in Banstead. He sold his business in 1999 and has now retired. In his early days, he was an excellent soccer player with Corinthian Casuals.

M.A. Lynch

RHB & ROBB, 1977-1994

Birth: Georgetown, British Guyana 21/05/1958

Matches: 304 *306*

Batting career for Surrey:

I	NO	HS	Runs
491	59	172*	15674
276	*34*	*136*	*6800*

Av	100s	1000s	
36.28	33	8	
28.09	*5*		

Bowling career for Surrey:

Balls	Runs	Wkts	Av	Best	5wl
1931	1251	24	52.12	3-6	-
563	*471*	*13*	*36.23*	*2-2*	*1*

Catches: 314 *118*

Tests: 0
ODIs: 3, 1988

Some batsmen are born to block, others to entertain the crowds. There is not the slightest doubt into which category Monte Lynch fitted. Over the years, he added a discipline to temper the reckless moments that terminated early innings too often, but the basic instincts did not change. Even in his most attentive knocks, Monte Lynch never foreswore his attacking shots or resorted to stroke-less defence.

Born in Georgetown, British Guyana, Monte Lynch was educated in England at Ryden's School, Walton-on-Thames, Surrey, and therefore qualified as an English player. He was nursed through the Surrey Young Cricketers and on joining the first team at the age of nineteen, scored an attractive 101, his maiden first-class century against the Pakistan touring team at The Oval in only his eleventh innings. He was a middle-order right-hand bat and off-break bowler and occasional medium-pace bowler in one-day matches.

One of his early innings was 141* against Glamorgan at Cardiff in 1982, scored off 78 balls in 88 minutes. He went to Pakistan with an International XI in 1981/82 and the next winter played for his native Guyana (formerly British Guyana). Going to South Africa with a 'rebel' West Indian XI in 1983/84, he was banned from Test match cricket and one-day internationals until the end of the 1987 season.

He played in three one-day internationals in 1988, and was run out in the first match without facing a ball. His chance of further international honours was sunk by a horrendous broken leg and dislocated ankle, suffered while playing football just before the start of the 1989 season, when he had appeared fitter and fresher than for many years.

His best season in England was 1985, when he scored 1,714 first-class runs. The consistency in his play between 1983 and 1985, when he averaged over 50 in two of these seasons, marked him as one of the leading batsmen in the country. The dreadful leg injury hampered him severely, and lesser men might never have made it through the seasons of 1989 and 1990, but he soldiered on with restricted movement and improvised technique, which culminated in a score of 172* against Kent. He received a well-deserved benefit in 1991 and played for Surrey until 1994. He then moved on to Gloucestershire in 1995.

In his career, he played in 359 first-class matches, scoring 18,325 runs at 35.17 with 39 centuries. He took 26 wickets at 53.76 and held 367 catches. After retiring from the game, Monte Lynch took up a post as a teacher at Guildford Royal Grammar School.

Birth: Kennington, London 14/05/1918

Matches: 376

Batting career for Surrey:

I	NO	HS	Runs
544	75	143*	10893
Av	100s	1000s	
23.22	7	2	

Bowling career for Surrey:

Balls	Runs	Wkts	Av	Best	5wI
287	180	4	45.00	1-10	-

Catches: 615
Stumpings: 147

Tests: 3, 1950-1955

Competent and consistent, Arthur McIntyre missed most of the big honours of the game through being contemporary with Godfrey Evans. He gained only three caps, two when Evans was injured and one as a batsman against Australia at Brisbane in 1950. Many thought that McIntyre was the better wicketkeeper day in, day out, but he was not as much of a showman as Evans.

McIntyre was born within a quarter of a mile of The Oval and at the age of eight was playing cricket at Kennington Road School. It was as a 'keeper that he was chosen to play for London Schools.

He joined the Surrey groundstaff in 1936 as a batsman and leg-break bowler and was in the Second XI that won the Minor Counties Championship. In 1938, he made his debut in the first team, but his career was cut short by the outbreak of war. During the war, he met up with the Bedser twins in the Middle East, who persuaded him to turn to wicketkeeping. In 1946, Mobey was the regular Surrey wicketkeeper, but McIntyre kept his place as a batsman/bowler and was awarded his county cap. With considerable help from Herbert Strudwick, McIntyre improved his work behind the stumps and at the end of the 1946 season, McIntyre became the Surrey 'keeper when Mobey retired.

That 1947 season was the first time he had kept wicket to Alec Bedser and Laker, and in a match against Essex at Chelmsford, there were no fewer than 33 extras in the Essex second innings. Surrey, set 340 to win, lost 5 wickets for 125 but partly thanks to McIntyre, who made 70, Surrey turned pending defeat into victory by two wickets. Two years later, McIntyre had his best season behind the stumps with 94 victims. He was a pivotal figure in the Championship-winning sides under Surridge and May, when the close fielding contributed so much to the team's success. His big year was 1955, when his benefit raised £8,500, and he almost completed the wicketkeeping double, scoring 927 runs and having 85 dismissals.

McIntyre had always been a useful batsman, and against Nottinghamshire in 1955, he scored 189 runs for once out. In the first innings, he made 110, taking only 108 minutes over his century, and in the second innings he made 79 not out, helping Peter May put on 149 runs in 57 minutes.

A damaged hand in 1956 threatened his place, but he came back in 1957 to play a full season with great success. In 1958, he captained the side occasionally when May was on Test duty and Bedser was sick. He formally retired that year, taking up the position of Surrey coach, but played a few more games for the team until 1963. He now lives quietly in retirement in Hampshire.

Birth: Warwick, Queensland, Australia 12/06/1883
Death: Imtafa, Malta 23/07/1915

Matches: 98

Batting career for Surrey:

I	NO	HS	Runs
158	11	176	4195
Av	100s	1000s	
28.53	7	3	

Bowling career for Surrey:

Balls	Runs	Wkts	Av
4380	2121	101	21.00
Best	5wI	10wM	
7-41	6	1	

Catches: 91

Alan Marshal was born at Warwick, in Queensland, Australia, the son of a Lincolnshire man who had emigrated there. He took to cricket at a fairly young age, playing at both the South Brisbane State School and the Brisbane Grammar School. He was a cricketer of unfulfilled promise. He had it in him to be great, but somehow he missed the heights that at one time seemed to be within his reach. A hitter of greater natural powers has seldom been seen.

He played for a time in grade matches in Sydney and had represented Queensland a few times before coming to England. He always showed distinct talent, his batting improving rapidly from the time he had the advantage of playing on turf wickets. In England, he soon made his mark, his form being so good that he was asked to qualify for Surrey in 1905. Whilst qualifying by residence, he made 2,752 runs at 56.16 for London County and took 118 wickets (average 16.41 runs each). The following year, 1906, his aggregates were 3,578 (average 76.12) and 167 (average 14.10) respectively.

He duly appeared for the county and at first Marshal did not do himself full justice in his new surroundings. In the 1907 season, he made over 1,000 runs for Surrey, but there was a certain restraint in his play. In 1908, he showed everybody all that he could do. He had a splendid season for Surrey, scoring 1,884 runs, with an average of 40, in all matches for the county and finishing second only to Hayward. When the season ended, his place among the great players of the day seemed assured. Apart from his batting, he was a good change bowler and in the field there was no one to match him. He could fill any place with credit and no catch, if reasonably possible, escaped his hands. The future looked bright indeed for him, but he never again reached the same level.

At the height of the 1909 season, the Surrey committee suspended him for a time and in the following year, they terminated his engagement. Marshal returned to Queensland and played cricket there, but without achieving anything particularly exceptional. As a bowler he had two great successes for Surrey at The Oval in 1908, taking 5 wickets for 19 against Nottinghamshire in the August Bank Holiday match. In the match against Derbyshire, at one period he dismissed five men in 13 balls without a run being made off him.

In the First World War, he served with the Australian Imperial Forces and went to Gallipoli. He died of enteric fever in a military hospital in Malta.

P.B.H. May CBE
RHB, 1950-1963

Birth: Reading, Berkshire 31/12/1929
Death: Liphook, Hampshire, 27/12/1994

Matches: 208

Batting career for Surrey:

I	NO	HS	Runs
327	46	211*	14168
Av	100s	1000s	
50.41	39	7	

Catches: 182

Tests: 66, 1951-1961

The most talented English batsman of his generation, May first came to the public eye whilst at Charterhouse, where he was in the XI for four years, heading the school's batting averages at the age of fourteen. In 1946, he represented Berkshire and, at the age of seventeen, hit a brilliant 146 for the Public Schools against Combined Services at Lord's.

Surrey claimed him through his school qualification and he made his first-team debut in 1950 whilst still at Cambridge University, having also played first-class cricket for Combined Services in 1948 and 1949. He started with two poor matches, but then scored one century and 3 fifties in the 11 Championship matches up to the end of the season. This greatly contributed to the team finishing as joint Champions with Lancashire in 1950, and he was awarded his county cap.

In 1951, he played only seven Championship matches, being at university, but scored three centuries (two in one match against Essex at Southend) and 2 fifties. He made his Test debut that year, scoring a century in his first innings against South Africa at Headingley, and finished top of the national averages.

In his last year at university, he formed a leading part in the Championship-winning side at Surrey, averaging 67. 00 for the county.

In his first full year for Surrey, 1953, he scored 5 centuries and 6 fifties to average 57 in Championship matches in the second year of Surrey's seven-year run of victories in the Championship. 1954 was not such a good season due to very wet weather, but on uncovered wickets, May showed his skill by scoring runs on pitches that defeated almost everybody else. For example, in 1955, at Weston-super-Mare, Tony Lock had the highest score on either side with 36, apart from Peter May, who scored 93. At the start of his career, fielding was not his strongest point, but he worked on it to become a good close fielder, which is reflected by the number of catches he held. In 1956, May had a relatively poor season overall, but had some excellent performances with Surrey despite his international calls.

He was appointed captain of Surrey in 1957 and had a remarkable season, retaining the Championship. It was in this year that he played his most famous Test match innings, in partnership with Colin Cowdrey against West Indies at Edgbaston. He scored 285* and virtually ended the mysteries of Ramadhin which had plagued English batsmen for years.

1958 was another outstanding season, being the last Championship-winning season for Surrey. In 1959, he started playing later in the season following his marriage and was taken ill in July, needing an operation for a serious digestive disorder which prevented him playing for the rest of 1959 and all of 1960.

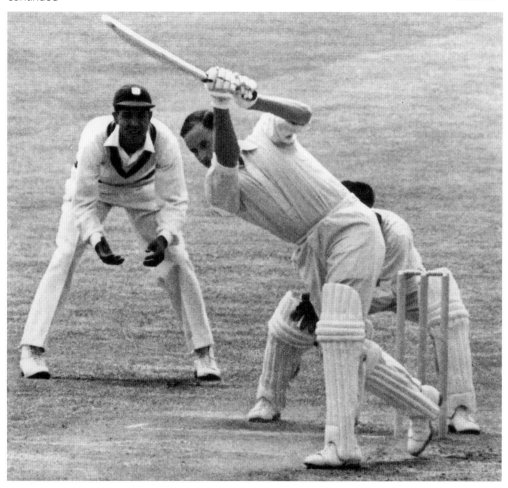

In 1961, he was in moderate form, missing a number of matches through injury and in 1962, having withdrawn from international cricket, he expected to play a full season for Surrey. However, business calls and injury meant he played only 17 of the 28 Championship games and was often out in the 40s and 50s. He retired from all cricket in 1963, playing only three games for the county.

He was considered by many critics and by his contemporaries as the finest batsman of his era, and he had an outstanding international career with 66 appearances, 41 as captain. In 1955, he was appointed captain to succeed Len Hutton, having had no captaincy experience since leaving school, but whilst captain he led his country to victory in 20 out of 41 matches.

What were his strengths as a player? He possessed intense, watchful concentration, which made him one of the best bad-wicket players ever seen. He invariably took the fight to the bowlers, always ready to attack and ready to drive the fast bowlers down the ground. He was a master of all strokes, using a bat no heavier than 2lb 4oz, but his glory was the on-drive, perhaps technically the most difficult of execution.

After his playing career was over, he concentrated on his business life, but was persuaded to become a Test selector and, for several years, was chairman of selectors, a position which did not sit easily with his character. Sadly, Peter May died in December 1994 after a short illness. He had been looking forward to becoming president of Surrey during the club's 150th anniversary in 1995.

K.T. Medlycott
RHB & LSB, 1984-1991

Born: Whitechapel, London 12/05/1965

Matches: 134 *56*

Batting career for Surrey:

I	NO	HS	Runs
173	37	153	3586
36	*9*	*44**	*379*
Av	100s	1000s	
26.36	3		
14.03	*-*		

Bowling career for Surrey:

Balls	Runs	Wkts	Av
21326	10726	331	32.40
1695	*1382*	*49*	*28.20*
Best	5wI	10wM	
8-52	17	5	
4-18	*3*		

Catches: 88 *15*

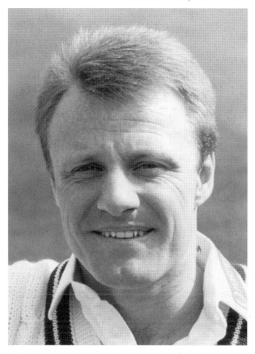

Keith Medlycott was born in Whitechapel in the East End of London and went to school on the Isle of Dogs – a true East Ender. At his first primary school there was no cricket, but he played football and was spotted by a teacher from another school in a district side match and moved to Sir William Burrough School for his last year in primary education. It was here that he was introduced to cricket, and he then went to Parmiters Grammar School in Wandsworth, where he took up spin bowling. He played club cricket with his father for Grove Park, Kent, and the City of London CC, where he received great encouragement from Tom Sheppard and Len Rangecroft. During a season with the MCC groundstaff, he was persuaded to join Surrey by Micky Stewart in preference to Northamptonshire, who had also offered him a contract.

In 1989, he took 69 wickets in the season at 24 apiece, the only English bowler to beat this was Vic Marks with 76 at 29. This included his best bowling performance of 8 for 52, against Sussex at Hove, which lead to a comprehensive win. He took 10 wickets in a match on three occasions. Keith was a good fielder and an unorthodox but effective bat at six, seven or eight. In 1987, he recorded his highest score of 153, batting at number eight, sharing a seventh-wicket stand of 262 against Kent at The Oval, a record highest stand for this wicket. Early on in his career, he tended to be aggressive in his bowling, but Ian Greig and the Surrey staff persuaded him to bowl more in the 'channel' to become a reliable member of the side.

Keith Medlycott went with the England team to West Indies in 1989/90 but did not play in the Test team. In three matches, he took 13 wickets from just over 100 overs. The following winter, he was in the England A party that went to Pakistan and Sri Lanka where he suffered a chronic loss of confidence, but nevertheless maintained great cheerfulness and mixed well with the opposition players in Sri Lanka. His last season for Surrey was in 1991, when the county finished fifth in the Championship.

Having played for Northern Transvaal in 1988/89, he returned to become their manager from 1995 to 1997, and then became manager and coach at Surrey. His record as manager must be the envy of all the other counties as in 1997, the Second XI won the Aon Risk Trophy and then the First XI lifted the County Championship in 1999, 2000 and 2002, also winning the Benson & Hedges Cup in 2001.

Birth: Battersea, London 23/04/1913
Death: Bromley, Kent 26/01/1983

Matches: 334

Batting career for Surrey:

I	NO	HS	Runs
512	70	255	14068
Av	100s	1000s	
31.82	20	9	

Bowling career for Surrey:

Balls	Runs	Wkts	Av	Best	5wl
35974	15387	538	28.60	6-34	8

Catches: 317

John (Jack) Frederick Parker played for Surrey from 1932 to 1952, his career spanning the last days of Jack Hobbs to the early days of Peter May. For years he was an essential member of the side, a consistent bat and a fine driver, whose instinct was to attack and many of whose best innings were played in a crisis. He was a medium-paced bowler, who could open if required, and who, without many sensational performances, was always getting wickets, and was a safe catcher in the slips.

A tall man, he would have done even better but for a troublesome back. It was often said that had he been given the opportunity of batting higher in the order during his early days, his batting would have blossomed even sooner than it did. He was basically a county player and, although he was picked for the tour of India in 1939 which never took place, one doubts that he would have established himself in Test cricket.

It is, however, fair to point out that the war deprived him of playing between the ages of twenty-six and thirty-three, when he might have expected to be at his best. He had a good trial in 1932 and 1933 and, without

doing anything exceptional, showed promise, but then came a setback. In 1934 he lost his place and he did little more until 1937, when he scored 915 runs, with an average of 27.72, and took 65 wickets at 28.36. In 1938 came his first century and, in 1939 he surpassed anything he had done before with 1,549 runs, at an average of 37.78, and 56 wickets at 22.83. This improvement was partly due to health, while in bowling he concentrated more on length and on always aiming at the stumps. But, overall, his best years were after the war.

In 1946, despite further trouble with his health, he headed the bowling averages with 56 wickets at 15.58 and followed up in 1947 by heading the batting. In 1949, he made the highest score of his career, 255 against the New Zealanders, made out of 568 in six and a half hours. In all, he had an average of over 50 against touring teams. He continued to be a valuable member of the Surrey side until 1952, when, although he was unable to bowl, he still scored his usual 1,000 runs. He retired at the end of the season, having had the satisfaction of playing in the first Surrey team to win the Championship since 1914. He had a benefit in 1951. In all first-class cricket he scored 14,272 runs, with an average of 31.58, including 20 centuries, took 543 wickets at 28.87 and took 331 catches.

Birth: Maidstone, Kent 06/10/1890
Death: Newbury, Hampshire 08/10/1961

Matches: 324

Batting career for Surrey:

I	NO	HS	Runs
411	50	200*	8497
Av	100s	1000s	
23.53	4	-	

Bowling career for Surrey:

Balls	Runs	Wkts	Av
53189	20261	778	26.04
Best	5wl	10wM	
8-60	30	1	

Catches: 176

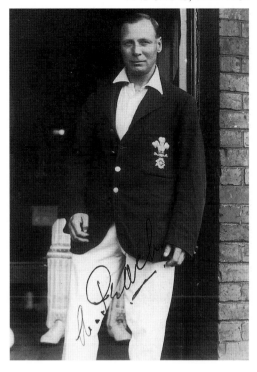

Herbert Peach was a more than useful all-rounder for Surrey from 1919 to 1931 – during this time he scored 8,709 runs, average 23.61, and took 785 wickets for 26.38 each. He played for the Second XI for two seasons before the First World War and made his first-class debut in 1919. Peach was a joyous cricketer, and his many hard-hitting runs gave much pleasure at The Oval in the 1920s.

This right-handed batsman had tremendous power and, on numerous occasions, he was the leading partner in lightning bursts of scoring, often in conjunction with P.G.H. Fender. In 1924, he hit balls from both Bates (Glamorgan) and Newman (Hampshire) clean out of The Oval, and at Swansea he scored 50 out of 56 in boundaries. At The Oval in 1928, he amassed 96 out of 129 in less than a hour against Hampshire, but his most famous innings and the highlight of his career was at Northampton in 1920. At a rate of more than a run a minute, he scored 200* (26 fours) out of 492 against Northamptonshire, adding 288 for the fifth wicket in two and a quarter hours with Andy Ducat and 171 for the sixth wicket in 42 minutes with Fender.

He was a naturally aggressive batsman, not cultured, but often devastatingly effective and, on one occasion at The Oval struck all six balls of an over to the boundary. Against Essex at Leyton in 1925, he scored 109 in 85 minutes. He was a medium-pace bowler who did a large amount of work for Surrey, mostly on perfect Oval wickets but always with an honest cheerfulness. As an untiring medium-paced bowler able to spin the ball, he did best in 1923 when his wickets numbered 83 at 23.15 apiece. The following season, he enjoyed the satisfaction of dismissing four Sussex batsmen with successive balls at The Oval, when off his next delivery a catch was dropped, which prevented him from achieving a unique feat. He finished with an analysis of 8 wickets for 60. A first-rate fieldsmen in any position, he held 167 catches. He never took 100 wickets in a season, coming closest in 1928 with 96, and just missing out on 1,000 runs in a season in both 1920 and 1925.

He played six times for the Players against the Gentlemen between 1923 and 1928, and in 1929 went on Julien Cahn's tour to Jamaica. When he was not re-engaged at the end of the 1931 season, he moved into Minor Counties cricket playing for Berkshire in 1933 and 1934. He returned to Surrey as coach from 1935 to 1939 and he was responsible for the discovery of the Bedser twins.

Birth: Bangor, Caernarvonshire 24/09/1946

Matches: 485 *315*

Batting career for Surrey:

I	NO	HS	Runs
503	144	75*	4400
156	*61*	*22*	*693*
Av	100s	1000s	
12.25	-	-	
7.29	*-*		

Bowling career for Surrey:

Balls	Runs	Wkts	Av
84625	35577	1399	25.43
14823	*8959*	*326*	*27.48*
Best	5wI	10wM	
9-57	53	7	
4-11	*7*		

Catches: 154 *58*

Tests: 25, 1967/68-1984/85
ODIs: 1, 1984/85

Pat Pocock played cricket at school and for Melton Cricket Club, progressing through to the Surrey and England Schools teams. Arthur McIntyre saw him playing for Surrey Schools and recommended him to the county.

Pat, or 'Percy', Pocock is a cheerful, open, friendly, talkative character and it was obvious from an early age that he had outstanding ability as an off-spinner. For Surrey he lies sixth in the all-time list of the bowlers who have taken the most wickets for Surrey. He created a sensation against Sussex at Eastbourne in 1972 by taking four wickets in five balls, then five in six, six in nine and finally, seven wickets in eleven balls. He took a second hat-trick against Worcestershire at Guildford in 1971. Over the years he was a consistent performer for Surrey, his best bowling figures being 9 for 57 against Glamorgan at Sophia Gardens, Cardiff, in 1979. In his last season, 1986, he was appointed captain of Surrey and, although they finished third in the Championship, his captaincy was not a particular success.

After playing for the Under-25 team, he made his England debut in the West Indies in 1967/68. He bowled impressively on the demanding pitches of the Caribbean, but was dropped the following summer despite taking 6 for 79 in the second innings of the first Test

against Australia. (Lawry had punished him in the first innings.)

He also went to Ceylon and Pakistan in 1968/69, Ceylon in 1969/70, India, Pakistan and Sri Lanka in 1972/73 and back to the West Indies in 1973/74. In the winter of 1984/85 he went with England to India and Sri Lanka. He also played for the Rest of World against Pakistan in 1970/71. He was surprisingly recalled into the England team for the Fourth Test at Old Trafford against West Indies in 1984, having last appeared eight years previously. He held his place for the remaining two Tests, and then played in all five Tests on the subsequent winter tour of India.

In the 1995 *Surrey Yearbook*, Pat said 'Nothing that I, personally, could have done could have given me greater pleasure, or introduced me to more lovely people, than playing cricket. One thing of which I am certain – that the game was infinitely harder to play at the end of my career than at the start.' After his retirement from the game, he served on the Surrey committee. Away from cricket, he is involved in golf marketing and golf travel.

Birth: Chepstow, Monmouthshire 13/02/1842
Death: Lambeth, London 18/07/1907

Matches: 256

Batting career for Surrey:

I	NO	HS	Runs
453	37	97	6642
Av	100s	1000s	
15.96	-	-	

Bowling career for Surrey:

Balls	Runs	Wkts	Av	Best	5wl
595	371	6	61.83	2-39	-

Catches: 357
Stumpings: 250

In 1862, Edward Pooley was engaged as one of the bowlers at The Oval, but his regular connection with Surrey did not begin until 1865. In the meantime, he played for Middlesex, making his first appearance against MCC at Lord's on 25 July 1864. The story of how he came to succeed Tom Lockyer is told by himself in *Old English Cricketers*. He said, 'My introduction to wicketkeeping would be about the year 1863. Old Tom Lockyer's hands were bad, and the ground being fiery he could not take his usual place behind the sticks. Mr. F.P. Miller, the Surrey captain, was in a quandary as to who should relieve him, I went up to him and said, "Mr. Miller, let me have a try." I donned the gloves, quickly took two or three wickets, and seemed so much at home that Tom Lockyer said I was born to keep wicket and would have to be his successor in the Surrey team. What he said came true.'

In 1866, Pooley established his position as one of the leading professionals of the day and remained a member of Surrey for seventeen years, finally dropping out in 1883. His great days as a wicketkeeper date from the time of James Southerton's connection with Surrey in 1867. It is safe to say that no wicketkeeper could have assisted Southerton to the extent

that Pooley did. He was quick as lightning and, with all his brilliancy, very safe. Partly from lack of opportunity, he was not quite so good to very fast bowling, but to slow bowling he was, in his day, supreme. His record of the greatest number of wickets obtained in a first-class match still stands after many years. In the Surrey *v.* Sussex match at The Oval in July 1868, he dismissed 12 batsmen, stumping four and catching eight. Apart from his wicketkeeping, Pooley was a first-rate bat, free in style, with fine driving power and any amount of confidence.

He made many good scores and would, without a doubt, have been a much greater run-getter if he had not been so constantly troubled by damaged hands. During the Canterbury Week of 1871, he played an innings of 93 when suffering from a broken finger. The faults of character that marred Pooley's career and were the cause of the poverty in which he spent the later years of his life are described in the book *His Own Enemy* by Keith Booth. He was, in many ways, his own worse enemy, but even to the last he had a geniality and sense of humour that, to a certain extent, condoned his weaknesses.

Birth: Thames Ditton, Surrey 09/02/1859
Death: Winchester, Hampshire 17/02/1929

Matches: 278

Batting career for Surrey:

I	NO	HS	Runs
450	35	186*	10840
Av	100s	1000s	
26.12	8	2	

Bowling career for Surrey:

Balls	Runs	Wkts	Av	Best	5wl
3355	1610	64	25.15	6-41	1

Catches: 163

Tests: 17, 1882-1893

During his career, which extended from 1880 to 1895, Maurice Read, nephew of the famous H.H. Stephenson, ranked among the best professional players and obtained all the chief honours that the cricket field had to offer. He earned his place in the Surrey XI at the first attempt and maintained his form to the end of his career. So that he could take up an appointment on the Tichborne estate, he retired after a season in which he made 1,031 runs, with an average of 31.

Always an enterprising player, Maurice Read had some unorthodox strokes, but these were natural to a forcing batsman of his style. He hit the ball hard in defence and could cut and keep down his off-drive with masterly ease. A rather fast bowler, he occasionally did useful work with the ball before George Lohmann and Jack Beaumont, under John Shuter's captaincy, made Surrey tremendously strong. In the deep field and at third man he was brilliant, having remarkably sure hands in picking up and catching, as well as being quick in getting to the ball. In 1886, playing for Surrey against the Australians, he made his highest score of 186*, sharing in a partnership of 241 with Bobby Abel.

He first played for England at The Oval in 1882, when Spofforth's bowling won Australia a sensational victory by seven runs. He was still in England's best side in 1890, when he appeared in the Test matches at The Oval and Lord's, and he also played at Lord's in 1893. He took a large share in winning the 1890 match at The Oval, when the Surrey authorities could not get together a fully representative XI. On a bowler's pitch, Australia were dismissed for 92 and 102, so England, after getting 100, wanted 95 to win. Four wickets fell for 32 runs, but Maurice Read, who made 35, and James Cranston took the score to 83 and England scraped home by two wickets.

Maurice Read went to Australia four times, in the winters of 1884, 1886, 1887 and 1891, taking part in 11 Test matches. His last trip was with Lord Sheffield's team, captained by W.G. Grace. The Test match played at The Oval in 1893 was played for his benefit.

In all matches, first-class and second-class, for the county he scored 13,058 runs, with an average of 26 and took 78 wickets for 22 runs each. After his retirement from great matches, he kept up with the game in Hampshire. Although qualified to do so by residence, having married the hostess of the Tichborne Arms, he never appeared for that county. In several seasons he averaged over 100 runs an innings for Tichborne Park.

Birth: Reigate, Surrey 23/11/1855
Death: Addiscombe Park, Surrey 06/01/1907

Matches: 366

Batting career for Surrey:

I	NO	HS	Runs
580	41	338	17683
Av	100s	1000s	
32.80	31	5	

Bowling career for Surrey:

Balls	Runs	Wkts	Av	Best	5wl
4547	2830	84	33.69	4-27	-

Catches: 302
Stumpings: 18

Tests: 18, 1882/83-1893

Affectionately known as 'W.W.', Walter Read was introduced to Surrey by Harry Jupp, and he made his debut at the age of seventeen, having played for Reigate Priory when thirteen years old. A cricketing future seemed assured, but he could not afford to play the game without remuneration, for he had no private income and his family could not support him.

During his first eight years for the county he only played during school vacations, as he helped his father run a school in Reigate. The obvious remedy of turning professional was simply not available to someone from a middle-class background, for to be a professional cricketer was not deemed suitable work for an educated man. The Surrey secretary, C.W. Alcock, came up with a solution, appointing him as assistant secretary at the club. The next few years were truly prolific for Read.

He made his first century in 1876 out of 588 runs for the season (average 42.20). Standing 5ft 11in tall, he was a middle-order batsman, a right-arm fast-round arm bowler and, later in his career, a slow under-arm bowler. An excellent point fielder, he quite often kept wicket.

His first century in representative matches, before Test matches started, was a score of 117 in less than two hours. Batting at number ten, for England against Australia at The Oval, he featured in a record partnership of 151 with Scotton. He toured Australia with Bligh in 1882/83 and Vernon in 1887/88, and led the tour to South Africa in 1891/92. He played in 10 Test matches from 1882 to 1893, and was captain twice.

His best domestic season was 1885, when he scored 2,384 runs (average 54. 18) with a highest score of 214*, and also scored 159 for Gentlemen v. Players at The Oval. He was the leading Surrey batsman for eight successive years from 1881 to 1888. Read still holds the record for the highest individual scores against the Universities with 244* against Cambridge in 1887 and 338 against Oxford in 1880, both at The Oval. In 1885 he scored eight centuries and in 1887 two consecutive 200s. He was at the height of his batting prowess in 1889 and still batted well in 1892 with four centuries. He was regarded as one of the best batsmen in England in the 1880s, scoring over 1,000 runs in nine seasons.

He was an all-round sportsman, playing association football, could skate well, excelled at billiards and won prizes for walking. He received a benefit in 1895 when he ceased being the assistant secretary, and retired from the game in 1897. He then had a modest career as an estate agent and auctioneer before returning to Surrey to coach young players from 1905 to 1907.

C.J. Richards

RHB, RMB & WK, 1976-1988

Birth: Penzance, Cornwall 10/08/1958

Matches: 256 237

Batting career for Surrey:

I	NO	HS	Runs
328	79	172*	7142
175	43	113	2727
Av	100s	1000s	
28.68	7	1	
20.65	3		

Bowling career for Surrey:

Balls	Runs	Wkts	Av	Best	5wl
270	219	5	43.80	2-42	-

Catches: 534 181
Stumpings: 66 49

Tests: 8, 1986/87-1988
ODIs: 22, 1981/82-1987/88

Raised in Penzance, Jack Richards was only interested in riding horses. At the age of thirteen a friend asked him up to the local cricket club and, eight years later, he was the regular wicketkeeper for Surrey. There was no history of cricket in the family, but his promise was so apparent at the age of sixteen that his father suggested he write to Middlesex and Surrey. At Middlesex, he attended pre-season nets, but Surrey gave him a week's trial which was followed immediately by a six month's contract.

On the tall side for a wicketkeeper at 5ft 10in, one of his strengths was his ability to stand up to medium-pace bowlers. As his career developed, his batting improved and he achieved 1,000 runs in a season in 1986. He made his debut in 1976, although he spent most of that year in the Second XI. In 1977 he played in 11 Championship matches, sharing the wicketkeeping duties with Leonard Skinner. However, he made the position his own in 1978, received his county cap and was the regular 'keeper for the county until 1988, sharing the 'keeping in later years with Alec Stewart.

He toured Australia and New Zealand with Derrick Robins' Under-23 team in 1979/80. In 1981/82 he made his one-day international debut for England in India playing in two matches there and one in Sri Lanka.

Selected for the England team to tour Australia in 1986/87, he made his Test match debut at Brisbane. At Perth, in his second Test match, he scored his only Test century with 133. At international level, there was intense competition for the wicketkeeping place from Bruce French, Bob Taylor and eventually Jack Russell.

Overall, he played in 8 Test matches and 22 one-day internationals, his last Test match being at The Oval against the West Indies in 1988. For Surrey, his wicketkeeping was of a high standard, twice taking ten dismissals in a match in the same season (1987). His batting in the middle order was consistent and included seven centuries, the highest being 172* against Kent at The Oval in 1987, when he shared in a record seventh-wicket partnership for Surrey with Keith Medlycott. In one-day cricket, he scored three centuries for Surrey, the most spectacular being 113* against Somerset, when his second fifty was scored off 27 balls.

At the end of the 1988 season, he was released on the recommendation of the cricket sub-committee with a year of his contract still to run. Married to a Dutch lady, he emigrated to Holland and played no more first-class cricket.

T. Richardson

RHB & RFB, 1892-1904

Birth: Byfleet, Surrey 11/08/1870
Death: St Jean D'Arvey, Savoie, France 02/07/1912

Matches: 305

Batting career for Surrey:

I	NO	HS	Runs
396	106	69	2853
Av	100s	1000s	
9.83	-	-	

Bowling career for Surrey:

Balls	Runs	Wkts	Av
64994	31732	1775	17.87
Best	5wI	10wM	
10-45	169	60	

Catches: 106

Tests: 14, 1893-1897/98

Tom Richardson played his first match for Surrey in May 1892 and was an immediate success, returning match figures of 12 for 100 at The Oval against Essex. However, it was not until 1893 that he gained a regular place. In that year, he played in the final Test against Australia and again made a spectacular debut, taking ten wickets in the match. Richardson's stock weapon was speed; he got the majority of his wickets through speed alone.

A strikingly handsome fellow, over 6ft tall, slim but muscular, with dark, curly hair, black moustache, low forehead, and black, penetrating eyes, he looked like a Mediterranean brigand. Yet in character and disposition he was the kindest and most sensitive of men. 'Honest Tom', they called him at The Oval, and they loved him for it. Straightforward as a man and as a bowler, he relied on his natural gifts for success. These included a high action, pace, accuracy, stamina and a phenomenal break-back and, unlike many great bowlers, he was not a hater of batsmen. With his natural body swing and break-back, he found it paid him to pitch the ball up and this may well have been the secret of the amazing frequency with which he hit the stumps.

He bowled most of his overs with an old, almost seamless ball, in the days before a new ball was taken in mid-innings. He took fifteen wickets in a Championship match five times and no other Surrey bowler has performed the feat more than twice. In four successive home seasons, he amassed over 1,000 wickets, a feat unparalleled for a fast bowler. Three times he took over 200 wickets in a season and in each of these seasons he bowled over 1,600 five-ball overs. Yet his stamina was so inexhaustible that batsmen swore he was as fast at the end of a day's play as at the start.

While he was at his best, from 1893 to 1897, Richardson scarcely knew what it was to be out of form. But he began to lose efficiency before he was twenty-eight and, although for a year or two longer he did bril-

and most legendary performance was at Old Trafford in 1896, when Australia took 84.3 overs to score the 125 they needed for victory. Richardson, bowling throughout, with 42.3 five-ball overs in three hours, took six of the seven wickets that fell. The picture painted by Neville Cardus of a heroic athlete forced in the end to admit defeat is one of the most poignant in all cricket. In the Test match at Lord's in the same season, he recorded one of his finest performances when he and George Lohmann bowled the Australians out on a perfect wicket for a total of 53. In that innings, Richardson bowled 11 overs and three balls for 39 runs and six wickets.

On the 1897/98 tour of Australia, he suffered a setback. Overweight and troubled by rheumatism, he was rarely the force he had been on the previous tour and in 1899, his benefit year, he failed to find a place in the England team. In 1897, Surrey missed out on the Championship by a whisker but is was no fault of Richardson's. He once scored 60 against Gloucestershire at The Oval, but he never took his batting seriously. His business was to get wickets and, with that end in view, he kept himself fresh, seldom staying in long enough to discount his bowling.

In January 1902, having cleared over £1,000 from his benefit, he became the landlord of the Cricketers' Arms at Kingston and this may have shortened his Indian summer. In 1903, at the age of thirty-three, Richardson took 119 wickets in the Championship and, despite being hampered by a wet season, his form was described as his best for many years. After a few matches in 1904, he was dropped. In an attempted comeback against the Australians in 1905, he made no impact and so in 1907 he became landlord of the Prince's Head on Richmond Green. There he remained until his untimely death five years later in 1912. His career record of 2,015 wickets at 18.42, 1,775 of them for Surrey, places him firmly among the greatest of the Surrey greats.

liant things, he was never again his old self. A great increase in weight rather than hard work was responsible for his comparatively early decline.

He played in 14 Test matches, all against Australia and took 88 wickets, a striking rate that is superior to that of any other international bowler before or since – fast, medium or slow. In his first tour of Australia in 1894/95, he took 32 Test match wickets, more than any fast bowler in Australia, until Larwood beat it by one nearly forty years later. His greatest

G.J.R. Roope
RHB & RMB, 1964-1982

Birth: Fareham, Hampshire 12/07/1946

Matches: 342 277

Batting career for Surrey:

I	NO	HS	Runs
554	118	171	16226
256	45	120*	6092
Av	100s	1000s	
37.21	22	7	
28.87	2		

Bowling career for Surrey:

Balls	Runs	Wkts	Av	Best	5wl
16132	7725	211	36.61	5-14	3
4817	3650	125	29.20	5-23	3

Catches: 513 127
Stumpings: 2 2

Tests: 21, 1972/73-1978
ODIs: 8, 1973-1978

Graham Roope's talent was soon recognised at Bradfield College and he played for the Public Schools against the Combined Services at Lord's. Before joining Surrey, he scored a century for Berkshire. For eighteen years Graham was in the Surrey team and his contribution as batsman, slip fielder and bowler was a great asset, particularly in the Championship-winning year of 1971 and the 1974 Benson & Hedges Cup success.

His talents were recognised by selection for England in 21 Tests and two tours. It is easy to be impressed by the likes of Ian Botham, but less easy to acknowledge the worth of a player who does the right thing at the right time for his side. For instance, there was an outstanding defiance lasting five hours on a bad pitch at Karachi, ended by an awful leg-before decision. There was a partnership with Bob Taylor to effect a recovery at Christchurch and, in the same match, a superb catch above his head at slip, which *Wisden* described as 'like a goal-keeper', which he was. (Graham's list of football clubs including Wimbledon, Kingstonians, Woking and Corinthian Casuals.)

In 1971 when Surrey were County Champions Graham took 59 catches. He scored five centuries and his aggregate was second only to John Edrich. He was described as Surrey's most enterprising batsman, excelling in the drive. How can you assess the merit of such a player by mere statistics? The same can be said of his Test career. His highest score of 77 was at The Oval against Australia when, it is almost unnecessary to add, England were in a tight position and needed the runs. Accordingly, his innings was worth many a century. He made seven half-centuries and thirty-five catches in Test matches.

Back with Surrey, there was an excellent century against the Australians. He was basically a front-foot batsman in the Tom Graveney mould, but a change in pace of pitches necessitated a back-foot technique. But he was not a slave to theory and, like all good batsman, he improvised successfully.

Graham, in full flow, was attractive to watch and difficult to bowl to, and he clearly enjoyed his cricket. Other highlights included a contribution to a Benson & Hedges Cup victory, and in eight seasons he exceeded 1,000 runs. He was a splendidly loyal Surrey player and a credit to the club on tour. He returned to Berkshire between 1983 and 1988; his last first-class match was for Minor Counties in 1986. Graham Roope now lives in West Yorkshire, where he is involved in coaching and commentating.

Birth: Cobham, Surrey 06/09/1880
Death: Ewell, Surrey 13/07/1962

Matches: 228

Batting career for Surrey:

I	NO	HS	Runs
289	129	58*	1192
Av	100s	1000s	
7.45	-	-	

Bowling career for Surrey:

Balls	Runs	Wkts	Av
44748	19544	954	20.48
Best	5wI	10wM	
10-43	58	9	

Catches: 64

Thomas Rushby was a celebrated medium-paced bowler for Surrey between 1903 and 1921. Born in Cobham, he attracted the attention of the county authorities with his performances for his local club and, as a result, was invited to become a professional at The Oval.

He made his debut in 1903, playing in both the First and Second XIs. After somewhat slow progress, he took 11 wickets for 74 against Buckinghamshire and 13 for 104 against Dorset in 1908, feats which heralded his greatest years.

Perhaps his finest season was 1909, with 119 wickets at an average of just over 16, including 10 for 88 against the Australians when Surrey won by five runs. In the same season, he took 5 for 28 in each innings against Derbyshire and 5 for 9 against Yorkshire at The Oval, when Yorkshire were dismissed for their lowest ever score against Surrey of 26. In 1907 at The Oval, he (6 for 67) and J.N. Crawford (11 for 63) bowled unchanged during the two innings of Sussex, who were disposed of for 43 and 90. Surrey won by an innings and 94 runs.

Following some friction with the Surrey club, he spent 1910 as a professional with Accrington in the Lancashire League, but returned to The Oval the following year, reaching his highest aggregate, 132 wickets, and appearing for Players against Gentlemen.

A right-arm fast-medium bowler who often formed a deadly combination with W.C. 'Razor' Smith, Thomas Rushby took 100 wickets in a season on four occasions and twice exceeded 90 in a year. He was still in great form after the First World War, taking 6 for 12 against Essex at Leyton in 1919, but the highlight of his career was 10 for 43 in 17.5 overs v. Somerset at Taunton in 1921. This was the last season of his first-class career, for ill health prevented him playing in 1922, though he was granted a benefit in the match against Kent at The Oval, with very successful results.

Twice he headed the Surrey averages – in 1914 with 103 wickets for 19.14 and in his last season, 59 wickets for 18.84 apiece. During his career, he took 954 wickets at 20.58.

He rarely achieved much as a batsman. However, he scored 58* against Worcestershire in 1909, going in last, out of a career total of 1,227 at 7.90. After he retired, he became a private coach.

I.D.K. Salisbury
RHB & RLBB, 1997-

Birth: Northampton 21/01/1970

Matches: 87 *84*

Batting career for Surrey:

I	NO	HS	Runs
109	18	100*	1890
54	*16*	*34**	*487*

Av	100s	1000s
20.76	1	
12.81	-	

Bowling career for Surrey:

Balls	Runs	Wkts	Av
14237	6344	242	26.21
3324	*2548*	*80*	*31.85*

Best	5wl	10wM
8-60	10	2
4-32	*2*	

Catches: 44 *32*

Tests: 15, 1992-
ODIs: 4, 1992-

Ian Salisbury is a rarity, an English leg-spinner and a successful one too at county level. He bowls well-flighted leg-breaks, has a well-disguised googly and generally maintains good length and line. Not a big spinner of the ball, he relies on variation of length and pace. A useful bat, he often contributes runs in the lower order without really being considered an all-rounder.

Ian Salisbury played his early cricket for the village of Brixworth, near Northampton, and played for Northamptonshire at junior levels up to the Under-19s. He made his first-class debut with Sussex in 1989, earning his cap in 1991. His best bowling performance for them was 8 for 75 against Essex at Chelmsford, and his highest score was 83 against Glamorgan at Hove.

His success was rewarded with a Test against Pakistan and he took five wickets in the match, but was unable to produce consistent performances at the highest level. He played twelve Tests over the next six years and toured India and the West Indies but failed to make an impact. A move to Surrey in 1997 revitalised his career, and joining Saqlain Mushtaq saw the formation of a very effective spin partnership.

Drifting away from the international scene, he spent his winters honing his craft in grade cricket in Australia, earning the Sydney Grade Player of the Year award in 1999/2000.

A superb county season in 2000 led to a recall to the England tour party for Pakistan in 2000/01. Unfortunately, he failed to make any impression on the Test series there, and was discarded for the 2001 tour of Sri Lanka.

In 2000, Ian Salisbury recorded his best bowling performance for the county, with 8 for 60 in one innings and 12 for 91 in the match against Somerset at The Oval. In the same season, he took eleven wickets in the match against Durham at The Oval. This very productive season saw him record his best one-day figures, with 4 for 32 against Essex at Colchester in the National League. He was very proud to have scored a first-class century when he made 100* against Somerset at The Oval in 1999.

His overseas tours include England A to Pakistan (1990/91), Bermuda and the West Indies (1991/92), India (1994/95), and Pakistan (1995/96). He also went with England to India, Sri Lanka 1992/93 and the West Indies in 1993/94. In addition, he played for the World Masters XI *v.* the Indian Masters XI in November 1996.

He enjoys coaching at Surrey's first cricket academy and when his cricket career is over, he intends to become a school PE teacher.

A. Sandham
RHB, 1911-1937

Birth: Streatham, London 06/07/1890
Death: Westminster, London 20/04/1982

Matches: 525

Batting career for Surrey:

I	NO	HS	Runs
830	71	292*	33312
Av	100s	1000s	
43.88	83	18	

Bowling career for Surrey:

Balls	Runs	Wkts	Av	Best	5wI
771	386	16	24.12	3-27	-

Catches: 129

Tests: 14, 1921-1929/30

Always remembered for his famous opening partnership with Hobbs, Sandham was a considerable batsman in his own right. One of only 24 men to have scored 100 centuries in a career, he made the first score of over 300 in Test cricket, 325 for England against West Indies at Kingston, Jamaica, in 1929/30. As a Surrey player, coach and scorer over a period of sixty years, from 1911 to 1970, he became a familiar and warmly respected figure to two generations of those who frequented Kennington Oval.

Neatly built, dapper, lean, wiry and quick-footed, 'Andy', or 'Sandy', was a quiet, unassuming, kindly man; but a determined competitor. His was an impeccable Surrey pedigree. Born in Streatham, he played for Streatham United and Mitcham before, in 1911, at the age of twenty, he joined The Oval staff and made his first county appearance in the same season. Having taught himself by watching Tom Hayward at The Oval, he had a straightness of the bat and was strong in playing the ball off his legs. Before the First World War, he struggled to find a place in the first team.

After the war, Sandham succeeded the man on whom he had modelled his batting and became Jack Hobb's opening partner for Surrey. In the ensuing fifteen years, they shared 67 century stands.

A cricketing idealist, firm in his principles, he was generous and modest with a dry, but warm sense of humour. If he ever resented being regarded as the junior member of the Hobbs-Sandham partnership, he never showed it. Indeed, he was always quick to extol the older man's human and batting merits.

Before Surrey's 1926 match with Oxford, one of the university officials hinted that they resented the county resting their better players from that fixture. As a result, Hobbs and Sandham were included. After the strong university side had scored 273, Hobbs and Sandham put on 428 for the first wicket in just over five hours. For a completely self-taught cricketer, Sandham was remarkably correct; eminently straight-batted, strong on his legs, a fearless hooker, a delicate and dedicated cutter and infallibly dextrous in deflection. He rarely bowled, but as a fielder in the outfield he was fast, brilliant and secure.

Sandham and Hobbs, of course, were famous for their sharp singles. He once said of that knack – with his wry grin – 'We never called; we just looked and went. I knew Jack wanted a run as soon as he shaped for his push on the off-side, and I was a yard or soon down the wicket as soon as the ball was bowled'.

Although he lost four years of cricket due to the First World War, only ten batsmen have ever exceeded his aggregate of 41,284 runs (average 44. 82 with 107 centuries). Yet, in a period vastly rich in opening batsmen, he played in only 14 Test matches (879 runs at 38.21). His overseas tours included going with MCC to South Africa in 1922/23, Australia in 1924/25, India, Burma and Ceylon in 1926/27, the West Indies in 1929/30; with Sir Julian Cahn to Jamaica in 1928/29; and with Brinckman to South America in 1937/38.

He carried his bat through an innings on seven occasions and twice scored a century before lunch. 1921 was an important season for Sandham as Hobbs, because of illness, only made one first-team appearance. He shouldered the responsibility well, scoring 1,914 runs. In the match against Essex, Andy dropped down to number eleven in the bat-ting order, having been unwell. Joining Ducat, they added 173 in 100 minutes before Sandham was run out for 58. Not suprisingly, this still stands as the highest tenth-wicket partnership for Surrey. He followed this with his highest score for Surrey of 292* against Northamptonshire at The Oval. His most productive year was 1929 with 2,565 runs (average 51. 30) of which 2,348 (53.36) were scored for Surrey.

In the years that Hobbs and Sandham played together for Surrey (1919 to 1934), Sandham scored 28,107 runs for the county from 655 innings (average 47. 31) and Hobbs scored 25,211 runs in 478 innings (average 58. 90). Other large partnerships in which he was involved include 299 for the second wicket, with Ducat against Lancashire at Old Trafford in 1928, and 298 for the sixth wicket, with H.S. Harrison against Sussex at The Oval in 1913, still a county record for that wicket.

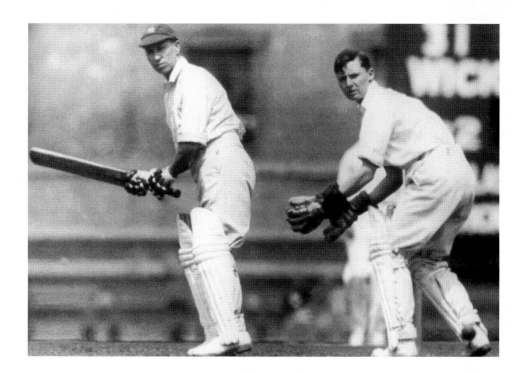

Saqlain Mushtaq
RHB & RLBB, 1997-

Birth: Lahore, Pakistan 27/11/1976

Matches: 58 72

Batting career for Surrey:

I	NO	HS	Runs
74	23	66	997
39	14	38*	282
Av	100s	1000s	
19.54	-		
11.28	-		

Bowling career for Surrey:

Balls	Runs	Wkts	Av
14232	5723	315	18.16
3368	2269	93	24.39
Best	5wl	10wM	
8-65	27	10	
4-17	4		

Catches: 22 / 5

Tests: [Pakistan] 40, 1995/96-
ODIs: [Pakistan] 156, 1995/96-

Saqlain Mushtaq was born in Lahore, the son of a government clerk, and his two elder brothers taught him the rudiments of the game. One, Sibtain, played at first-class level for Lahore and instructed his younger brother in off-spin, while Zulqamain helped with his batting. By the age of thirteen he was an all-rounder in the Zariff Memorial Club Second XI. It was always off-spin for Saqlain.

A new-age off-spinner who loves variation, Saqlain Mushtaq has mastered a mystery ball that spins away from the batsman although it is delivered with an off-spinner's action. He calls it the 'doosra', Urdu for 'the other one'. He has a fast, short-stepping action with a halting delivery and has a propensity to bowl no-balls, unusually for a bowler with such a short run. Saqlain has been criticised for attempting too much variation, and he often throws in the 'doosra' the first time a batsman faces him. He has adhesive qualities as a batsman and has shared in several lower-order stands, even making a dogged Test hundred. With Alistair Brown, he shared in a tenth-wicket partnership of 141 against Leicestershire at Oakham in 2000.

Saqlain made his first-class debut in 1994/95, aged seventeen when he took 52 wickets in his first season and was picked to represent Pakistan 'A' in a one-day tournament in Dhaka. Full international recognition came quickly, and he made his Test debut in September 1995 in Peshawar, where he took four wickets, followed by five in the next match. During the World Cup of 1999, Saqlain claimed 17 wickets, but time has not lessened the pain he felt when Pakistan lost the final to Australia.

Saqlain joined Surrey in 1997, a step which he considers to have been wholly beneficial. He made an immediate impact, taking ten wickets in a match in both his fifth and sixth first-class games for the county. With Ian Salisbury, Surrey have the most effective spin partnership in the country, and in his six years with the county, Saqlain has averaged more than five wickets in each Championship game, a record that has not been surpassed in the last one hundred years. Pakistan have benefited from his fine performances over the year, having first call on his services, but Saqlain is always back to play for Surrey at every available opportunity, being a loyal and enthusiastic member of the team.

Birth: Ruddington, Nottinghamshire 09/12/1866
Death: Ruddington, Nottinghamshire 19/06/1936

Matches: 59

Batting career for Surrey:

I	NO	HS	Runs
79	27	36	503
Av	100s	1000s	
9.67	-		

Bowling career for Surrey:

Balls	Runs	Wkts	Av
11226	4183	275	15.21
Best	5wI	10wM	
9-47	19	6	

Catches: 35

Tests: 3, 1890-1891/92

John William Sharpe was born in Ruddington, Nottinghamshire. His father, Samuel Sharpe, played two games for Nottinghamshire, but for many years was professional for Rock Ferry, where John Sharpe served his apprenticeship on the cricket field. His first engagement, with the Bedford Town Club in 1884, was sufficient to prove his capacity as a promising all-rounder. In 1886, he received trials for the Colts against the county at Trent Bridge. On one occasion, he took four wickets for five runs, but there was not room for him in the very powerful Nottinghamshire XI of those days, and so Sharpe qualified by residence to join Surrey at Kennington Oval.

Playing for Surrey from 1889 to 1893, he took 462 wickets at 13.81 runs each in all matches for the county. His best year was 1890, when altogether 179 wickets fell before him at just over 12 runs apiece. Next season, in the match with Middlesex at The Oval, he dismissed 9 men for 47 in the first innings and 5 for 50 in the second. Against Lancashire, at Old Trafford in 1890, and the following year against Somerset at The Oval, he and Lohmann bowled unchanged through both innings. His best bowling performance was against Middlesex, again at The Oval, in 1891, when he took 9 wickets for 47.

Sharpe, with a beautiful easy action, bowled especially well on hard pitches, and could make the ball break from the off to a remarkable degree for a man of such pace; his extra-fast 'yorker' was deadly. Although handicapped by the loss of his right eye in childhood, Sharpe was a smart fielder and often proved a useful batsman, notably on his first appearance for Surrey, when he helped George Lohmann put on 149 runs for the last wicket against Essex. Later in the season, he and Beaumont going in at number eleven made 118 together. The next match after the Essex game was against Oxford University when, in twenty-one overs and one ball, he dismissed five batsmen, all of them clean bowled at a cost of only two runs.

In 1890, he played for England against Australia at The Oval, and, in the autumn of 1891, he went to Australia with the team organised by Lord Sheffield. After returning from Australia, Sharpe lost his form and, although he appeared for Nottinghamshire in 1894, his first-class career practically ceased when he left Surrey. At that time, Surrey were exceptionally strong. From 1887 to 1895, they only once fell from first place in the County Championship.

Birth: Headington Quarry, Oxfordshire 05/12/1889
Death: Norbiton, Surrey 13/02/1957

Matches: 354

Batting career for Surrey:

I	NO	HS	Runs
520	60	277*	18254
Av	**100s**	**1000s**	
39.68	41	12	

Bowling career for Surrey:

Balls	Runs	Wkts	Av	Best	5wl
35133	13478	439	30.70	6-78	12

Catches: 267

Tom Shepherd was one of Surrey's great batsmen just after the First World War, a time when the county were richly endowed with run-getters and a place in the side was extremely difficult to command. He played for Surrey from 1919 until 1932, when he retired and became head groundsman and coach to Wandgas CC, in Wandsworth, a post he held until his death. In all first-class cricket, Shepherd hit 18,719 runs, including 42 centuries, at an average of 39.82, took 441 wickets at 30.81 and generally fielding in the slips, held 274 catches.

His rise to fame was sensational. In 1920, he provided almost the entire batting strength of the Second XI. He hit 236 from the Essex Second XI bowling at Leyton and altogether scored 709 runs, average 101.28. As he also took 38 wickets, average 15.50, he headed both sets of averages. These performances literally forced Surrey to give him a regular position in the Championship team and he seized his opportunity with such avidity that in each of eleven successive seasons he exceeded 1,000 runs.

In 1921, he had a sudden jump to fame as Hobbs was out of the side with injury. He distinguished himself by hitting 212 against Lancashire at The Oval, and 210* against Kent at Blackheath, then known as 'The Surrey Graveyard', in the following innings. Shepherd scored 1,658 runs in the season, including six centuries, in Champion-ship fixtures, averaging 51.81.

In 1923, he was excellent without quite achieving all that was hoped of him. By 1924, although a little uneven in form, he had some very fine innings, but scarcely any other batsman of that time depended so largely upon hard driving. He did even better in 1927, putting together eight centuries with 277* against Gloucestershire at The Oval being the highest. In the course of his innings, which was the biggest of his career, occupying four and three-quarter hours, he and A. Ducat put on 289 in two and three-quarter hours for the fourth wicket. Shepherd's aggregate that summer reached 2,145 at 55.00, of which 1,681 were registered in Championship matches. The previous season, he hit two separate centuries in a match – 121 and 101* from the Leicestershire attack at The Oval.

Born at Headington Quarry near Oxford, Shepherd played for his village team at the age of eleven. A player of imperturbable temperament, he suited his methods to the conditions and the state of the game, for while he could pull and hit to the off with exhilarating power, he was also capable of considerable patience. He appeared in Test trial matches and for Players against Gentlemen, but so great was the competition at the time that he never played for England.

Birth: Mitcham, Surrey 01/12/1825
Death: Croydon, Surrey 10/10/1911

Matches: 51

Batting career for Surrey:

I	NO	HS	Runs
81	19	32	422
Av	100s	1000s	
6.80	-	-	

Bowling career for Surrey:

Balls	Runs	Wkts	Av
5160+	1781	125	14.24
Best	5wI	10wM	
8-?	20	7	

(plus 107 other wickets)

+figures not available for 11 matches from 1847 to 1853

Catches: 32

Tom Sherman was one of the fastest round-armed bowlers of his era and, for some seasons, he was very successful in the Surrey team, also being a fine fielder. He was reported as batting in a good style but was too impatient, often running in at the ball and trying to make it a 'half-volley'. His first match for Surrey was in 1847 and the last in 1870, spanning twenty-five years. In all matches, he obtained 229 wickets and scored 422 runs with an average of 6. 91.

He first took ten wickets in a match against Kent at Aylesford in 1847, and consistently took five wickets in an innings for Surrey. In 51 matches for the county, he took five wickets or more in an innings twenty times. His purple patch came in 1851, when on four occasions, he took more than ten wickets in a match against Middlesex, MCC, Nottinghamshire and Yorkshire, and then repeated the feat against Yorkshire at Sheffield. When the South beat the North at Tunbridge Wells in 1855, he and John Lillywhite, bowling unchanged throughout, dismissed the North

for 77 and 74, Sherman taking eight of the wickets for 71 runs. However, his greatest feat was to obtain six wickets for 16 runs for Surrey and Sussex against England at Lord's three years earlier.

Standing 5ft 9½in, his pace was described as fast, quicker than most bowlers of his day, very straight and apt to whip off the bails with a really fine ball which seemed unplayable.

Sherman was also secretary to the New All-England XI. A block-cutter by trade, he lived in Mitcham. After his great days he coached at several colleges and schools, including Harrow, Eton, Winchester and Rugby and to the close of his long life, he continued to take a great interest in the game. He belonged to a cricketing family, both his father (James Sherman) and an uncle (John Sherman) having played for Surrey in their time. It may be of interest to recall that the latter was born at Crayford, Kent, on 14 October 1783, and that his father, old Tom's grandfather that is, was fetched away from a cricket match for the event. The name was originally Shearman.

Birth: Thornton Heath, Surrey 09/02/1855
Death: Blackheath, London 05/07/1920

Matches: 274

Batting career for Surrey:

I	NO	HS	Runs
447	19	135	9369
Av	100s	1000s	
21.89	8	0	

Bowling career for Surrey:

Balls	Runs	Wkts	Av	Best	5wl
84	37	0			

Catches: 141

Tests: 1, 1888

The name of John Shuter will be remembered as long as the Surrey club exists, as it was under his leadership that Surrey won back the first place among the counties in 1887 and enjoyed for the next five seasons a period of unequalled success. John Shuter belonged to Surrey by birth, being born at Thornton Heath but living at Bexley, he was in his young days connected with club cricket in Kent. He was in the Winchester XI from 1871 to 1873, being captain in his last year.

After leaving Winchester, John Shuter played in a county match for Kent in 1874 and in the following year, he played for the County XI against the Kent Colts at Catford Bridge. However, his potential value as a batsman was not realised and, after a time, he threw in his lot with Surrey, playing three matches in 1877. He had no success in that year, but in 1878 he took a very decided step forward and left no doubt as to his class.

The season of 1886, marked by a double victory over the Australians, saw Surrey being considered as nearly as good a side as Nottinghamshire, and in 1887 came the full reward of long-continued effort. For the first time since 1864, Surrey stood at the top of the tree. John Shuter had long before this made himself a first-rate captain, and he had a splendid team under his command. Once on top, Surrey did not look back until 1893. They were first in 1888, tied with Lancashire and Nottinghamshire in 1889, and were first in 1890, 1891 and 1892.

There came a decline of fortune in 1893, but as some compensation for falling behind in county cricket, Surrey won both their matches with the Australians. After the season of 1893, Shuter, to everyone's regret, was compelled by the stress of business to resign the captaincy. In thinking of John Shuter as the Surrey captain, one is apt to forget what a fine batsman he was, good enough for any team. For so short a man, (he was only 5ft 6in), he had a singularly graceful style and his punishing power on the off-side was remarkable. He did not care for averages or personal glory. His one idea was to win the match for his side.

John Shuter played nine times for the Gentlemen against the Players, but with little success, his best score being 41. All his best work was done for Surrey. He played once for England against Australia at The Oval in 1888. In the long years between his resignation of the captaincy and his appointment in 1919 as secretary of the club, he was always in close touch with Surrey cricket.

W.C. Smith
RHB & ROBB, 1900-1914

Birth: Oxford 04/10/1877
Death: Bermondsey, London 15/07/1946

Matches: 229

Batting career for Surrey:

I	NO	HS	Runs
318	62	69*	3193
Av	100s	1000s	
12.47	-		

Bowling career for Surrey:

Balls	Runs	Wkts	Av
42709	17616	1036	17.00
Best	5wI	10wM	
9-31	92	27	

Catches: 144

Born in Oxford, William Smith came to London to play for Crystal Palace. When that team turned into the London County Club, Smith came to the attention of W.G. Grace, who spoke about him to the Surrey committee. Indeed, Smith stated frankly that he owed nearly everything to 'W.G.'.

Being extremely thin brought William Smith the affectionate nickname of 'Razor' and he lived up to the description by getting much 'cut' on the ball. The off-break brought most of the 1,061 wickets in his career, which he took at an average cost of 17.45. His career might have lasted longer than from 1900 to 1914, but for his frail physique and weak heart, the cause of his death. This occurred at Surridge's, the famous bat makers and the firm with whom he was associated for many years. Owing to this weakness, he seldom played through a full season, but when equal to the strain of much work, he seldom failed, and if helped by the state of the pitch, he carried all before him. He took most of his wickets, not with the right-handed bowler's ordinary off-breaks but with the quicker ball that went away with the arm. It did not, as a rule, break much, but pitching on the leg stump did just enough to beat the bat. Moreover, it was so accurate in pitch as to be very difficult to hit.

He never made many runs with the bat, but his first century in first or second-class county cricket was no less than 201, for Surrey Second XI against Buckinghamshire at Reigate.

In 1909, he and Rushby dismissed Yorkshire for 26, the smallest total ever recorded by that county. In 1905, when the Australians won by 22 runs, 12 wickets fell to Smith for 124 runs and he earned identical figures for Surrey against the touring side of 1909. Most success came to him in 1910, when he was credited with 247 wickets at 13.06 each, Colin Blythe of Kent being next best with 175. In County Championship matches, he took 215 wickets at 12.56 each, bowling more than twice as many overs as any one of his colleagues. Against Northamptonshire at The Oval, he returned astounding figures: 14 wickets at a cost of 29 runs in 28 overs, and when batting he also scored 31*, only Ducat, with 67, making more in the match.

Accurate length, deceptive flight and swerve from leg helped to make him extremely difficult to play. It was said at the time that, for Surrey, no slow bowler could be compared to Smith since James Southerton, some fifty years before. He was honoured deservedly with a place in the Players team at Lord's in 1910, and in 1912/13 toured the West Indies with MCC. He was coach at Surrey from 1926 to 1928.

J. Southerton
RHB & R(RO)B, 1854-1879

Birth: Petworth, Sussex 16/11/1827
Death: Mitcham, Surrey 16/06/1880

Matches: 152

Batting career for Surrey:

I	NO	HS	Runs
261	77	82	1665
Av	100s	1000s	
9.04	-	-	

Bowling career for Surrey:

Balls	Runs	Wkts	Av
42223	13791	995	13.86
Best	5wI	10wM	
8-34	115	29	

Catches: 109

Tests: 2, 1876/77

James Southerton first played for Surrey in 1854, at the age of twenty-six, and then again in 1855. He played 70 matches for Sussex between 1858 and 1872 and 13 matches for Hampshire between 1861 and 1867. He played for all three counties in one season qualifying by birth for one and by residence for the other two. In June 1873, the county qualification rules were introduced and Southerton settled for Surrey as he was the landlord of The Cricketers at Mitcham, being known as the 'Mitcham Figaro'.

A typical tail-end batsman and slow right-hand round-arm bowler, he then played the bulk of his games for Surrey, but also played for Buckinghamshire in 1867. He went to Australia with W.G. Grace in 1860 (not first-class) and with Lillywhite in 1876/77, taking part in the first two recorded Test matches. He was 49 years and 119 days old, becoming the oldest player to make his Test debut. These were his only Test matches. He took seven wickets for 107, his best performance being 4 for 46.

Southerton took his first wicket in first-class cricket in 1860 (at the age of 32) and, seven years later, took 123 wickets in a season. In 1870, he was the first bowler to take over 200 wickets in a season with 210 at an average of 14.63. The previous year, he had taken four wickets in five balls against Lancashire at The Oval. He was involved in many notable matches. On 14 May 1872, he took 4 for 5 and 7 for 28 as MCC were bowled out for 16 and 71, with Surrey, 49 and 39 for 5, winning the match in a day.

Three years later, again at Lord's, he was instrumental in ending another match in a single day. Playing for the South against the North, he took the first nine wickets to fall at a personal cost of 30 runs. W.G. Grace ran out the last man. In the second innings, Southerton took 7 for 22.

Despite all his efforts and outstanding talent, Southerton's magnificent career coincided with one of the leanest periods in the Surrey club's history. In his first-class career, he took a total of 1,681 wickets at 14.44, taking ten wickets in a match on 59 occasions and five wickets in an innings 192 times.

A late developer, his craft and cunning matured with age. Standing 5ft 6in, he was stocky and strong with thoughtful and twinkling eyes, and played until 1879, after which he was appointed superintendent of the ground bowlers at The Oval. His term of office was brief as he died in June 1880 at the age of fifty-one. He was buried with great ceremony in Old Mitcham churchyard.

Birth: Kingston-on-Thames, Surrey 22/02/1909
Death: Richmond, Surrey 24/01/1950

Matches: 402

Batting career for Surrey:

I	NO	HS	Runs
643	44	236	18636
Av	100s	1000s	
31.11	36	11	

Bowling career for Surrey:

Balls	Runs	Wkts	Av	Best	5wI
22371	10496	297	35.34	8-52	7

Catches: 137

Stan Squires died in his forty-first year from an illness brought about by a virus in the blood. On leaving school at the age of sixteen, Squires began a business life in a City stock-broker's office but, contrary to his father's wishes, he always wanted to take up cricket as a profession. He spent his leisure time receiving lessons from Aubrey Faulkner, the South African Test player, and he joined Faulkner's coaching staff when a member of Richmond CC. Leading county cricketers noticed his ability and, in 1928 and 1929, he appeared for Surrey as an amateur making his debut in first-class cricket against Middlesex at Lord's. In 1930, he realised his ambition when Surrey gave him a contract as a professional and no more popular player wore the Surrey colours.

A perfect stylist, Squires was a model batsman for boys to copy. He possessed a rich abundance of strokes and best of all was his drive through the covers. He never appeared to impart any force into his batting; correct timing and supple wrists sent the ball speeding to the boundary. He was a grand fielder, notably in the deep and at cover. As a slow bowler, he specialised in off-breaks, although in later years he turned to the leg variety to suit his county's needs.

During the war, he served with the RAF, reaching the rank of Flying Officer. After spending two years in the Hebrides, he returned to this country wearing contact lenses (having always worn glasses before) which he used for boxing, squash, rugby and association football as well as cricket.

Between 1928 and 1949, Squires scored over 19,000 runs in first-class cricket and hit 37 centuries. His highest innings was 236 for Surrey against Lancashire at The Oval in 1933. He took his benefit in the Middlesex match at The Oval in 1948. He was at the top of his form in the summer preceding his death, when he made 1,785 runs with an average of 37.18.

During the winter Squires kept himself fit playing golf and, only a week or two before his fatal illness, he won the 27-hole foursome handicap in the Croydon and District Alliance competition for his club, Fulwell. Stan Squires was a licensee at Hampton Hill, and on his death left a widow and three children.

H.D.G. Leveson-Gower paid this tribute: 'Squires was an extremely good player, probably better than most people imagined. Often he scored runs when others failed. He was a great example to other professional cricketers. It is because of players like Squires that the profession to which they belong incites so much admiration.'

Birth: Esher, Surrey 03/05/1833
Death: Uppingham, Rutland 17/12/1896

Matches: 179

Batting career for Surrey:

I	NO	HS	Runs
312	24	119	5338
Av	100s	1000s	
18.53	2	-	

Bowling career for Surrey:

Balls	Runs	Wkts	Av
7629	3342	191	17.49
Best	5wI	10wM	
7-58	12	3	

Catches: 91
Stumpings: 11

Heathfield Harman Stephenson began to play for Surrey in 1853, having been a professional at Surbiton, and he took his benefit at The Oval in 1871, the year in which he retired from active pursuit of the game. In 1860, he was engaged by Broughton Club at Manchester, but he stayed for only one season.

He was the son of a doctor and as such was socially superior to many other professionals but he could not afford to adopt amateur status. He habitually wore a long frock coat, which gave him an ecclesiastical appearance. A tall man, he was a first-rate bat, being a strong, driving batsmen but, like so many big men, he was no cutter. He was second only to Lockyer as a wicketkeeper in his generation and kept in many of the All-England XI matches, Lockyer of the United All-England XI being among the opposition. During his first few seasons, he was a most effective bowler, almost unique in his ability to break the ball back with a round-arm action. Eventually, his fingers lost their snap. For the All-England XI, Stephenson is credited with the first hat-trick in cricket history at Sheffield against Hallam and Staveley in 1858, for which he was presented with a hat by his team-mates.

As a batsman, he perhaps reached his highest point in 1864, the last year until 1887 in which Surrey stood first among the counties. In 1864, he added 123 for the seventh wicket with Lockyer against Nottinghamshire, a record at that time, and with Mortlock put on 169 for the seventh wicket in the Players v. Gentlemen match at The Oval. He was the only player to score two centuries that season.

Apart from his merits as a player and a coach, Stephenson will be remembered as the first man to captain England in Australia in the winter of 1861/62, where he was regarded as the first of England's captain/ambassadors. He also toured Canada and the USA in 1859 (not first-class). In his first-class career, he played in 256 matches, scoring 7,360 runs at an average of 17.90, took 302 wickets at 16.40 and had wicketkeeping dismissals of 152 catches and 25 stumpings. He was certainly one of the most popular cricketers of his day.

Eventually, he joined Caesar on the umpires' list and stood in the first Test match ever played in England in 1880. In 1884, as a distinguished elder statesman among the professionals, he spoke out against the increase of throwing, which led to a change in the law and which curbed the abuse for a decade. He finished his days by coaching at Uppingham School for nearly a quarter of a century.

A.J. Stewart MBE
RHB & WK, 1981-

Birth: Merton, Surrey 08/04/1963

Matches: 260 *316*

Batting career for Surrey:

I	NO	HS	Runs
417	48	271*	14565
296	*37*	*167**	*9628*
Av	100s	1000s	
39.47	26	5	
37.17	*14*		

Bowling career for Surrey:

Balls	Runs	Wkts	Av	Best	5wl
455	401	3	133.66	1-7	
4	*8*	*0*			

Catches: 375 *269*
Stumpings: 12 *30*

Tests: 122, 1989/90-
ODIs: 155, 1989/90-

The rise of Alec James Stewart to the position of England vice-captain, acting-captain and genuine Test-class batsman has surprised many. It is not that the pedigree was absent: that Micky Stewart, the former Test player and Surrey captain, is his father is common knowledge. Less well known is the fact that his mother, Sheila, was a top netball and hockey player. It was a family environment always likely to produce a young sportsman.

His cricket progress was through the ranks. Tiffin School, junior Surrey sides, the Surrey Second XI during his final school year and, finally, when he left school at eighteen, he actually made it on to the Surrey staff.

Simultaneously, he began an association with Australian grade cricket at the Midland-Guildford club in Perth. Alec calls Perth his second home and credits it with being the finishing school for his cricket education. He played grade cricket from 1980 to 1989 and was such a fixture that they named a stand after him at their Lilac Hill ground.

If his batting skills were learned at The Oval, it was the Aussie school of hard knocks that instilled in him a mental toughness and a desire to give as good as he got. So, on his first tour, and

playing only his second Test, he crossed swords with Desmond Haynes at Trinidad – Haynes by no means got the better of him.

No one can say that success has come easily. He has always appeared to be a well-organised, busy, bat-twirling player, perky and capable of making entertaining runs, but lacking, apparently, the commitment to register the big scores that get noticed. The first ten years of his career brought him just 16 first-class centuries. Had he not developed his wicketkeeping, he might not have received his chance in international cricket.

Yet, even having made the squad, it was not easy to establish himself. Time after time he played fluently and well, getting set at the crease, only to waft once too often and depart, muttering to the sky. Dropped after the disastrous tour of Australia in 1990/91, he was recalled, much to his surprise, to keep wicket in the final Test against West Indies that summer. It was an opportunity he could not afford to miss and he took it. England won memorably. Two weeks later, he scored his first Test century against Sri Lanka and in the 17 Test innings after his return, he scored 952 runs at an average of 68.00.

Over the years, Stewart has filled a plethora of roles. He was vice-captain to Atherton and

Gooch, and captained the side himself for the first time against India in 1993. He was officially appointed captain in 1998 and led England for 14 Test matches altogether, including a series victory at home against South Africa. He also skippered them in the 1999 World Cup, standing down afterwards. He has batted in all positions from number one to number seven without complaint, for the good of the England side. At Bridgetown, in 1994, he became the first Englishman to score a century in each innings against the West Indies, scores of 118 and 143 steering England to victory. His highest score of 190 came against Pakistan at Edgbaston in 1992. Originally drafted into the squad as a batsman come wicket-keeper in an all-rounder role, he is now accepted as a wicketkeeper of international standing. By the end of 2002, he had played in 122 Test matches, the most recorded by any English player. There is an air of authority about his cricket.

He has been a consistent performer for Surrey, maintaining a batting average of around 40, with 26 centuries, his most successful years being in the late 1980s and early 1990s. In one-day cricket, his average is 37.17, second only to Mark Ramprakash and Graham Thorpe of the current squad. When not keeping wicket, he is an excellent fielder, both close to the wicket and in the outfield.

He was appointed captain of Surrey in 1992, and led the team to victory in the Benson & Hedges Cup final of 1994. Whilst remaining club captain, he handed over the team captaincy to Adam Hollioake in 1997, due to his increased international commitments.

M.J. Stewart OBE

RHB, 1954-1972

Birth: Herne Hill, London 16/09/1932

Matches: 498 74

Batting career for Surrey:

M	I	NO	Runs	
I	NO	HS	Runs	
844	91	227*	25007	
71	2	101	1151	
Av	100s	1000s		
33.20	48	14		
16.68	1	-		

Bowling career for Surrey:

Balls	Runs	Wkts	Av	Best	5wl
80	48	1	48.00	1-4	-

Catches: 605 24

Tests: 8, 1962-1963/64

Michael John Stewart was born in Herne Hill, London, and educated at Alleyn's School; he was, and is, very much a Londoner through and through. From his young days, Stewart took naturally to cricket. He played his first organised games at Dulwich Hamlet School, then went to Alleyn's School where he held his place for four years in the First XI and captained the side in his last two seasons. In his schooldays, he was a forcing batsman, going in number three or four, a splendid fielder and a fairly competent off-spin bowler. Selection for the two big public schools games at Lord's in 1949 and 1950 were the landmarks of his school career.

National Service followed. Torn between whether to go to university or to make sport his living, Stewart had his mind made up for him when B.H. Valentine, the former Kent captain, asked whether he would like to come to Kent after leaving the Army. Stewart had long toyed with the idea of becoming a professional cricketer and he told Valentine that he would be pleased to throw in his lot with Kent, if Surrey had no objections. After he appeared for the Army against the RAF at Lord's, Surrey decided to offer him a position on the playing staff for the 1953 season.

His career as a professional cricketer was one of gradual, but marked progress. Surrey promoted him to the county XI in 1954 and he demonstrated his potential in no uncertain manner by scoring 301 runs in his first four innings. He began with 52 and 6 against Gloucestershire and then hit 109 against Pakistan and 134 off Essex. His first season, 1955, yielded him 1,000 runs and his county cap. The following season his aggregate went past 1,500 runs, including his highest score, 166 against Essex, and, in 1957, he scored 1,801 runs at an average of 36.75. Having joined the invincible Surrey side of the 1950s part way through its triumphant procession of Championship titles, his contribution to that success was often crucial. Then followed the 1960s, which were not so swinging for Surrey, before an improvement, culminating in the 1971 Championship win under his diligent and astute captaincy, a grand climax to a long and glorious career.

He played first-class cricket in some or all of 21 seasons. In fifteen of these years, he scored over 1,000 runs – a remarkable display of consistency. In his career, he hit 49 centuries, of which 48 were made for Surrey, and he scored a century against every county, except Worcestershire, where his highest score was 83.

Micky Stewart often opened the batting for Surrey and figured in 83 century partnerships, 23 of those being with John Edrich. In 1962, he scored 2,045 first-class runs at an average of 44.45, of which 1,883 were scored for Surrey at an average of 44.83.

He was one of the best catchers the game has ever seen. In his first-class career, he took 634 catches, an average of 1.2 per game, and for Surrey, he took 605 catches in 498 games for the same average. In 1957, he pouched 77 catches, just one catch behind the all-time record of 78 held by Walter Hammond. At Northampton that year, he caught seven in one innings, a record which has since been equalled but has not been surpassed. Six of these catches were at short leg. Stewart's agility and enthusiasm as a fielder sprung from his imitation and admiration of Constantine. A cover-point at school, Stewart, under the guidance and discipline of Stuart Surridge, who insisted on fielding excellence, graduated to positions close to the wicket.

Micky Stewart was vice-captain of the club during Peter May's reign and was captain from 1963 to 1972. He was involved in the early days of the one-day game, playing 46 matches in the Sunday League and 4 in the Benson & Hedges competition. His Test match career consisted of only eight matches, four of which were against the strong West Indies side of 1963, where his highest score was 87.

Stewart's other sport, soccer, gave him enjoyment first as an amateur with Wimbledon, Hendon and Corinthian-Casuals and then as a professional with Charlton Athletic. He gained an amateur international cap for England against France in 1956.

After retiring from the game in 1972, he worked as a marketing manager for a sports company before being invited back by Surrey in 1979 to take up the position of cricket manager. This led to a similar position for the England team. In 1998, he was appointed president of Surrey CCC. He remains closely involved with both Surrey and the ECB.

Birth: Worthing, Sussex 06/01/1941

Matches: 315 / 123

Batting career for Surrey:

I	NO	HS	Runs
468	58	164	10402
113	7	56	1552
Av	100s	1000s	
25.37	12	5	
14.64	-		

Bowling career for Surrey:

Balls	Runs	Wkts	Av
34863	12903	490	26.33
5129	3119	115	27.12
Best	5wI	10wM	
8-22	11	2	
5-35	2		

Catches: 319 / 41

In 1963, John Arlott wrote, 'Stuart Storey had, to some extent, curbed his earlier impetuosity, to come into the team and win himself a place. He plays his strokes smoothly and easily, with time to spare; and when his selection of the ball to hit improves a little further, 1,000 runs per season, perhaps far more, should be within his scope. His ability to bowl at medium pace could simplify the whole question of team balance.'

This prophecy was quite accurate as Storey reached 1,000 runs in a season in five of the fifteen years he played for the county, and took five wickets in an innings eleven times in first-class matches and twice in one-day matches.

He was rarely out of any match, without making some either important contribution with the bat or ball, and sometimes as a slip fielder. When in full cry, he could be a spectacular batsman. His progress for Surrey built up slowly from 1960 to 1963 and he then became a stalwart member of the side until his retirement in 1974. He scored his first century in 1962 against Somerset at Taunton. His best bowling performance came in 1965, when he took 8 for 22 in the second innings against Glamorgan at Swansea, after taking three wickets in the first innings to give him ten wickets in a match for the first time.

In 1966, he became the first player for Surrey since Freddie Brown (in 1932) to achieve the double of 1,000 runs and 100 wickets. This was the only season in which he took more than 100 wickets and included 5 for 76 against Nottinghamshire at Trent Bridge and 6 for 100 against Kent at Blackheath. Ten wickets in a match against Glamorgan at Cardiff was the highlight of the year, with five wickets in each innings. The following year, he narrowly failed to achieve the 'double', but in a good year he scored 940 runs and took 78 wickets.

In 1968, he suffered a leg injury, which did not clear up fully until 1970. In 1971, he made his highest-ever score of 164 against Derbyshire at The Oval. As the years progressed, his bowling was less effective, 1967 being the last year that he took more than 50 wickets in a season.

He was awarded a benefit in 1973 and the following year was the only Surrey player to score a century. Storey made two in fact, one against Derbyshire at Chesterfield and the other against Essex at Ilford. In one-day cricket, his best bowling performance was against Middlesex in 1964 when he took 5 for 35 in the Gillette Cup. From 1979 to 1986, Stuart Storey was the coach at Sussex, having played 16 first-class matches for them in 1978.

Birth: Mitcham, Surrey 28/01/1880
Death: Shoreham, Sussex 14/02/1970

Matches: 554

Batting career for Surrey:

I	NO	HS	Runs
695	197	93	5485
Av	100s	1000s	
11.01	-	-	

Bowling career for Surrey:

Balls	Runs	Wkts	Av	Best	5wI
66	60	0			

Catches: 1035
Stumpings: 186

Tests: 28, 1909/10-1926

On his retirement, Herbert Strudwick held the world record for the most dismissals in a career by a wicketkeeper, but he now stands third in the all-time list. One of the greatest and assuredly one of the most popular players of his time, he helped to dismiss 1,497 batsmen, 72 of them in Test matches.

It is of interest to note that a lady set 'Struddy' on the path to becoming the world's most celebrated wicketkeeper. As a choirboy at Mitcham, he took part in matches under the supervision of the vicar's daughter, a Miss Wilson. Then about ten years old, Strudwick habitually ran in from cover to the wicket to take returns from the field. Observing how efficiently he did this, Miss Wilson once said: 'You ought to be a wicketkeeper.' From that point, Strudwick became one. His first club was Mitcham Wanderers and, at the age of sixteen, he received a postcard inviting him to The Oval for trials. He played for Surrey Colts in 1898, and then Surrey Club and Ground and the Second XI, before making his first-team debut in 1902.

Strudwick figured regularly behind the stumps for Surrey for twenty-five years, and afterwards became scorer from 1946 to 1957, thereby serving the county altogether for sixty years. He played 28 times for England, only 7 times at home, between 1911 and 1926 during the period when Australia and South Africa were their only Test match opponents. He would doubtless have been chosen more often, had he not been contemporary with A.A. Lilley, of Warwickshire, a better batsman. He toured Australia four times (1903/04, 1911/12, 1920/21 and 1924/25) and South Africa twice (1909/10 and 1913/14). He had tough bowlers to take in the form of Parkin, Douglas and Maurice Tate, but no one could have done the job better. The little man from Surrey stood right up to the fast bowler and made remarkably few mistakes. Very often he was right off the ground when the ball crashed into his gloves in front of his doubled-up body, and it was like the sound of a whip cracking. For England, at Johannesburg in 1913/14, he dismissed seven South African batsmen in the match. His best performance in a single innings was six catches against Sussex at The Oval and his best tally in a match was eight victims (seven caught, one stumped) against Essex at Leyton, both in 1904.

No more genuine sportsman, in every sense of the word, than the teetotal non-smoking Strudwick ever took the field for Surrey. An idol of the Surrey crowd, he was always ready to proffer helpful advice to young players. He never appealed unless sure in his own mind that a batsman was out and such was his keenness to save runs that he was frequently known to chase a ball to the boundary. Much of his greatness passed unnoticed because he was never the showman. He was a joker and a storyteller, enjoying life and travel, taking advantage of his touring days to see the world, and he certainly loved his cricket. He was also a great friend of Jack Hobbs.

He featured as one of the *Wisden* Five Cricketers of the Year in 1911, and received two benefits from Surrey in 1912 and 1924 – the latter at the age of forty-four. In the First World War, he was refused entry into the Army as he was too old, but he went on to serve in the RNAF (Royal Naval Air Force) for the duration of the war.

Not generally regarded as much of a batsman, he hit 93 in 90 minutes (easily his largest innings) against Essex at The Oval in 1913, when he and H.S. Harrison shared an eighth-wicket partnership of 134. In the second Test match at Melbourne, during the 1920/21 Australian tour, he distinguished himself with innings of 21* and 24. Strudwick could always command his place in a team on his wicket-keeping ability alone.

Honours bestowed upon 'Struddy' included honorary membership of MCC in 1949 and life membership of Surrey. S.C. Griffith, MCC secretary and a former England wicket-keeper commented: 'This wonderful man and great cricketer taught me, when fourteen, all I ever knew about wicketkeeping at the cricket school he helped to run in South London. He was the best coach I have ever known and from that time I numbered him among my dearest friends. Apart from his ability, he was one of the outstanding figures and personalities of the game.'

W.S. Surridge

RHB & RFMB, 1947-1959

Birth: Herne Hill, London 03/09/1917
Death: Glossop, Derbyshire 13/04/1992

Matches: 254

Batting career for Surrey:

I	NO	HS	Runs
316	32	87	3697
Av	100s	1000s	
13.01	-	-	

Bowling career for Surrey:

Balls	Runs	Wkts	Av
30675	13753	464	29.64
Best	5wI	10wM	
7-49	19	1	

Catches: 361

The grandfather of Stuart Surridge was a maker of cricket bats and violins, setting up his own business in the 1870s. In due course, Stuart was to become the owner of the family firm. Stuart was educated at Emanuel School, Wandsworth, where he kept wicket until he tried his luck as a fast bowler, the school being in dire need. This proved to be a good move on his part. He captained the school team in 1935 and also played for the Surrey Young Amateurs. In 1937, he first played for the county Second XI and made his debut for the full county side in June 1947, when Alec Bedser was on Test match duty. In 1948, he took the new ball when Bedser was away and his performances were good enough to secure him a permanent place in the side.

When Michael Barton retired at the end of the 1951 season, Surridge was invited to take control of the side which had an abundance of talent yet seemed unable to produce consistent results. When the captaincy was confirmed, it is said that he wrote in his diary, 'Surrey will win the Championship in the next five years.' If he did write this, he was right, although the Championship was not only won in the next five years but won for seven years in a row with five under his captaincy. It is for his captaincy that he will always be remembered, even though as a cricketer he was demonstrably more than an average performer, especially as a close-to-the-wicket fielder. Like an earlier Surrey captain,

Percy Fender, he controlled every game. Many of his decisions seemed eccentric at the time, but when proved correct only added to his reputation as a forceful and inspirational leader. One match in particular demonstrates his style. In 1954, against Worcestershire at The Oval, the visitors were dismissed for a mere 25 and, just as Surrey were building a commanding lead, he declared at 92 for 3 and then Surrey bowled Worcester out for 40. He had telephoned for a weather report for the following day and knew that rain was likely.

It must be said that for much of the time he was captain, Surrey were not the most popular side in the county Championship, but then how many winning teams are? At times the aggression shown by the close fielders was greater than many felt to be acceptable. Perhaps this was one reason why he was never chosen to captain any representative sides when he had so much to offer.

To win the County Championship for the five seasons of his captaincy is an achievement that is never likely to be equalled. He was fortunate in having around him bowlers of the calibre of Alec Bedser, Laker, Lock and Loader and batsmen such as May and Barrington, so technical ability was always available. As has been shown so often, mere ability is not enough, and a leader is needed to direct such undoubted talents. This was Stuart Surridge's achievement,

and in those five years Surrey won 86 and lost only 20 of the 139 Championship matches they played. Always one of the team, he travelled with his players and stayed at the same hotel, a style that was none too popular with the county committee. If he was hard on his players on the field, all was forgotten at the close of play.

The ability to fashion Surrey's diverse and flowing abilities into one effective force proved to be the rare gift of a natural leader. The Surridge approach was dynamic. Others have achieved this for a season, but Surridge did it for five years in a row and, what's more, he left a side as strong, if not stronger, than when he started. Fielding standards became almost unreal. Modern fielding is accepted as the last word in competence and athleticism, but Surrey under Surridge must still be the ultimate yard-

stick. Without a helmet in sight, Surrey supported their unmatched attack with zeal and efficiency and many an unfortunate batsman, knowing his first half-mistake would be his last, must have thought the natural laws of justice were being roughly overthrown. Surridge had hands like buckets, a fearless disposition and he would never ask any fielder to do what he was not prepared to do himself.

When he retired, he continued to serve the club, spending many years on the committee and becoming its president in 1982. He died in April 1992 whilst visiting one of his factories in Glossop in Derbyshire. His widow, Betty, became the first lady to hold the office of president. She wrote in the 1997 Surrey Year Book of her experiences during those never-to-be-forgotten years from 1952 to 1956.

Birth: Surbiton, Surrey 06/04/1934

Matches: 142 *8*

Batting career for Surrey:

I	NO	HS	Runs
131	64	24*	483
2	*0*	*8*	*8*
Av	100s	1000s	
7.20			
4.00			

Bowling career for Surrey:

Balls	Runs	Wkts	Av
25309	9548	481	19.85
528	*262*	*13*	*20.15*
Best	5wI	10wM	
9-70	26	3	
4-6	*1*		

Catches: 52 *3*

Growing up in the Tolworth area, David Sydenham played cricket from an early age for various clubs, ending up with East Molesey. He took many wickets as a schoolboy and then became an *Evening News* colt, which took him to the Gover Cricket School at Wandsworth from whence he graduated to the staff at Surrey. He took time to establish himself in the First XI, being in and out, mainly out, of the team. For the first five years, his up-and-down left-arm medium bowling tended to waywardness of direction and shortness of length.

His early opportunities came in 1958 when Alec Bedser and Peter Loader were absent from the team. He took 23 wickets in 8 matches, including 6 for 56 against Kent at The Oval. Playing in only five matches in 1959, David Sydenham still took more than five wickets in an innings on three occasions. Few wickets came his way in 1960, but things improved in 1961, with a best performance of 5 for 102 against Derbyshire.

His career centred on five seasons from 1961 to 1965, and he took more than 100 wickets in 1962 and 1963 when he usually opened the bowling. In 1962, he made the most of his unusual and naturally difficult angle of delivery, pushed the ball further up to the bat and made it move about late and sharply. He finished second in the first-class averages, and not surpris-

ingly topped the Surrey averages. He took 115 wickets that year at an average of 17.65. A golden spell in July saw him take five wickets in an innings in three consecutive matches against Kent, Worcestershire and Middlesex.

In 1963, he was again top of the Surrey averages taking 107 wickets at 15.85, his best analysis being 8 for 67 against Hampshire at Southampton. Although 1964 found him taking less than 100 wickets in the season, he was still first in the Surrey averages. He recorded his personal best performance of 9 for 70 against Gloucestershire at The Oval with twelve wickets in the match. His wicket haul was only 65 in 1965 and he dropped to second in the Surrey averages, but these included 7 for 32 against Yorkshire at Bradford and two five-wicket hauls in an innings against Somerset and Lancashire. He only played in eight one-day matches, but in his first match he took four wickets in five balls against Cheshire at Hoylake. He played in the Gillette final in 1965.

He made no more appearances for the Surrey first team after 1965 until a single appearance against Cambridge University at Fenner's in 1972. He retained his interest in cricket and was a member of the general and cricket committees for many years.

Birth: Farnham, Surrey 01/08/1969

Matches: 166 215

Batting career for Surrey:

I	NO	HS	Runs
272	36	222	10602
202	31	145*	6883
Av	100s	1000s	
44.92	29	4	
40.25	8		

Bowling career for Surrey:

Balls	Runs	Wkts	Av	Best	5wI
1879	1112	22	50.54	4-40	-
499	450	12	37.50	3-21	-

Catches: 133 89

Tests: 77, 1993-
ODIs: 82, 1993-

Graham Paul Thorpe was born into a sports-mad family and, by the age of thirteen, he was playing for Wrecclesham, a village team in the heart of Surrey. Two years later, he followed his brothers into the Farnham first team in the Surrey Championship and, at sixteen, he was invited up to The Oval. Cricket, though, was only half of it for Thorpe as he took a PE diploma at Farnham Sixth Form College and was a highly promising footballer, playing for the England Under-18s. Considering his future career, only Brentford had shown interest in his football, so cricket won the day. Micky Stewart and Geoff Arnold shaped his early development at Surrey, and his role models were doughty opener Ray Alikhan and left-arm spinner Keith Medlycott, who is now back at The Oval as coach.

A dependable and technically sound left-hander, he is capable of hitting, but also knows the value of ones and twos to keep the scoreboard ticking over. He was a stalwart batsman for Surrey throughout the 1990s, but since 1998 his appearances for the county have been rarer due to the much increased international programme. In one-day cricket for Surrey, he has maintained an average over 40, no mean feat. His occasional bowling has proved extremely useful in tight situations.

Only two years after his debut for Surrey, in 1988, he was selected to go on an England A tour to Zimbabwe and Kenya. The following three winters were spent touring with the A team to Pakistan, the West Indies and Australia. It proved an excellent way of gathering the experience necessary for the step up to Test level, which came in 1993. He announced himself with a second-innings 114*, and was the first England player in twenty years to score a century on debut. By 1997, he had something of a reputation as a 'nearly man'. Since scoring a century on his Test debut, he had reached 50 on 20 further occasions in 33 more Tests, but had only once made it through to three figures again. However, three centuries came in the next four Tests; two against New Zealand and one against Australia, which soon changed this perception. Even in an Ashes series that brought more disappointment for England, Thorpe topped the home batting with an average of 50.33, while none of his colleagues could even reach the 40s. To round off his summer, he signed off with a career-best 222 in the vital Championship match against Glamorgan.

An undemonstrative demeanour while batting hides a steely resolve, never more apparent than when he hit the winning runs while making an unbeaten 64 in the gloom of Karachi to clinch England's series win in Pakistan in 2000.

In Sri Lanka, he stirred himself to even greater efforts. In the deciding Test, he scored an unbeaten 113 when the next highest England score in the first innings was 26.

Thorpe's 2001 domestic season was ruined by injury. He began in splendid form, scoring 80 and 138 against Pakistan in the first two Tests. He also showed his value as a fielder, taking some marvellous catches in the slips. He suffered a calf strain, and when returning for the second Test against Australia, he was hit on the hand by Brett Lee, broke a bone and was out for the rest of the season.

In 2001/02, against New Zealand at Christchurch, he was dropped second ball when on four, but went on to record his personal best in Tests with an unbeaten double hundred.

Furthermore, it was the fourth-quickest double hundred of all time. Thorpe reached the end of 2002 with a Test average of almost 42. England's Test sides are invariably stronger for the presence of Graham Thorpe in their midst.

Graham Thorpe risked his international career by pulling out of England's tour to South Africa in 1999/2000 to spend time with his children, after touring for ten consecutive winters. But England needed his consistency and he was recalled the following summer. Involved in acrimonious divorce proceedings, 2002 saw Graham play little cricket and he withdrew from the winter tour to Australia. Our hopes are that he returns to full cricket in 2003 for both Surrey and England.

A.J. Tudor
RHB & RFB, 1995-

Birth: West Brompton, London 23/10/1977

Matches: 59 56

Batting career for Surrey

I	NO	HS	Runs
80	18	116	1348
37	8	29*	311
Av	100s	1000s	
21.74	1	-	
10.72	-		

Bowling career for Surrey

Balls	Runs	Wkts	Av
8381	4961	195	25.44
2481	1877	79	23.75
Best	5wl	10wM	
7-48	11	0	
4-26	3		

Catches: 15 / 13

Tests: 9, 1998/99-
ODIs: 3, 2002

Alex Tudor has all the natural attributes of a fast bowler; height, strength and the ability to bowl fast and extract bounce from most wickets. His talent was recognised early, and he played for London Schools at all levels from Under-8s. He won selection for the England Under-15 trip to South Africa in 1992/93 and played against India in 1994 for the Under-17 team. He also represented the Under-19 side, including a tour to Pakistan in 1996/97.

Making his first-class debut, against Middlesex at Lord's in 1995, as a seventeen year old, he soon impressed. He struck a maiden 50 against Leicestershire and took 5 for 32 against Derby. The only cloud on the horizon was his breakdown through injury in what was just his fifth game, an incident that was to become something of a recurring theme. Form and fitness deserted him in 1996, and he failed to break into the Surrey team.

Tudor was selected for the Ashes tour of 1998/99 after an indifferent season. In his Test debut at Perth, he took 4 for 89 and played in one more Test match on the tour. In the next home series, he scored 99* against New Zealand at Edgbaston, the highest-ever score by an English nightwatchman. Career-best figures of 7 for 48 in 2000 against Lancashire at The Oval, saw him called up for the England tour to Pakistan that winter, but he remained on the fringes of the side before travelling to the West Indies with England A, where he enjoyed a good tour.

A maiden first-class century at the start of 2001, 116 against Essex at The AMP Oval, saw his return to the England side, but his only significant contribution was 5 for 44 at Trent Bridge, his best Test figures to date. In the winter of 2001/02, he joined the first ECB National Academy Squad under the tutelage of Rodney Marsh, and a consistent start to the 2002 season for Surrey was rewarded with an England recall. At Old Trafford, he was Man of the Match after taking seven Sri Lankan wickets in the contest, but after making his one-day international debut, he fell victim to shin splints.

A tall man, 6ft 5in, with an imposing frame, hard work in the gym has increased Tudor's build fairly substantially. Capable of lateral movement with the ball, he tends to bowl within himself and rarely operates at full speed. A patient but hard-hitting lower-order batsman, his back-foot drive bears the hallmark of real class. A powerful thrower of the ball, he has developed into a reliable fielder for such a big man. The future beckons.

Waqar Younis
RHB & RFB, 1990-1993

Birth: Vehari, Pakistan 16/11/1971

Matches: 45 56

Batting career for Surrey:

I	NO	HS	Runs
47	16	31	447
24	6	39	152
Av	100s	1000s	
14.41	-	-	
8.44	-		

Bowling career for Surrey:

Balls	Runs	Wkts	Av
8722	4420	232	19.05
2796	1874	111	16.88
Best	5wI	10wM	
7-33	20	4	
5-26	8		

Catches: 11 9

Tests: [Pakistan] 80, 1989/90-
ODIs: [Pakistan] 248, 1989/90-

Waqar Younis only played for Surrey for three seasons, 1990, 1991 and 1993. In 1992, he played for Pakistan who were touring England. However, his impact during that time was sensational, taking a total of 343 wickets in all competitions. An astonishing number of Waqar's wickets have been clean bowled or have come from leg-before decisions. His strength lies in a deadly combination of explosive pace and late swing with which he has regularly been able to shatter the stumps or bruise the toes of apparently well-established batsmen. He took his wickets in 1991 despite generally slow pitches at The Oval and the fact that county batsmen had been alerted to his most potent deliveries after encountering him in 1990, his first season. Surrey have long since been grateful for Ian Greig's haste in signing Waqar after a solitary net and a fulsome recommendation from Imran Khan.

Waqar is an immensely physical bowler. There is about him the aggression of an impassioned warrior. At delivery, he jumps high and, pulling his arm through, he hurls himself at the batsmen, often finishing his follow-through just yards from his enemy and still breathing fire.

He was born in Burewala in the Vehari area of the Punjab, the breeding ground of so many courageous fighters; he was raised in Sharjah, where his father was a contract worker. Returning to Pakistan in his adolescence, Waqar played in obscurity until he was noticed by Imran Khan while bowling in a televised local knockout game. He took the seventeen year old under his wing and played him in Sharjah and in the Nehru Cup in 1989/90, before giving him his Test debut against India. He also included him in the team for Australia, where his surging pace made an impression.

Imran refined Waqar's run and action and taught him the fundamentals of swing, thus unleashing on the cricket world a bowler of exuberance and danger. When Waqar arrived at The Foster's Oval, it did not take long for everyone to realise that there was something very special about him. He has the ability to bowl at pace and also to swing the ball both ways, very late, which both batsman and wicketkeeper find difficult to stop.

In limited-over internationals, he recently passed the 400-wicket milestone to join his opening partner of many years, Wasim Akram, in that club.

Birth: Croydon, Surrey 10/02/1961

Matches: 155 224

Batting career for Surrey:

I	NO	HS	Runs
244	34	294*	8078
197	30	112	5066
Av	100s	1000s	
38.46	16	2	
30.33	5		

Bowling career for Surrey:

Balls	Runs	Wkts	Av	Best	5wl
107	113	2	56.50	2-66	-

Catches: 120 99
Stumpings: 3 3

Born in Croydon, David Ward went to Haling Manor School, was cricket captain at the age of twelve and played for Croydon Schools. He entered club cricket with Chipstead, making the First XI by 1978 and playing some games for Surrey Club and Ground. In 1982, he moved to Banstead, played for Surrey Young Cricketers and was offered a three-month contract by Micky Stewart. This was followed by a full contract in 1983.

Standing 6ft 1in tall, Ward was an attacking right-hand batsman, and on his debut in the John Player League in 1984, he scored 91 in two innings without being dismissed. He gained his Second XI cap in 1985. On his first-class debut, he scored 143 against Derbyshire at Derby and his career began to take shape by 1988 when he played in 25 matches, scoring 942 runs (average 31.40). 1990 was his best season when he became the twelfth Surrey player to score more than 2,000 Championship runs in a season, which included a new third-wicket county partnership record of 413 with Darren Bicknell, against Kent at Canterbury. He was then awarded his county cap. He volunteered to keep wicket whilst Alec Stewart was on Test duty or injured. Although not considered the best 'keeper, he filled the position well and was often used in one-day matches. David Ward had difficulty holding his place in the first team during 1992 and 1993 but came back in 1994 to record his highest score of 294*, a declaration robbing him of the chance to score a triple century.

A very popular cricketer, he contributed many useful innings in the one-day game including six centuries. He wielded his 2lb 14oz bat to murderous effect, beating the finest attacks into submission. In the long, slow build-up to the start of a match, you would see him taking time out to have a knock-up with the youngsters, or leaning over the picket fence for a chat with the members. That went a long way into making him something of a people's champion.

Earlier in his career, he played for Caulfield, Melbourne, from 1984 to 1987 and, in 1992, he went on the MCC tour to Leeward Isles, scoring the only 100 of the tour in Montserrat.

He retired from the first-class game at the age of thirty-five, returned to Banstead and also appeared for Hertfordshire in Minor Counties cricket. He is now a PE teacher and cricket coach at Whitgift School and it is thanks to his efforts that Surrey play one-day matches at the school, with a four-day county match planned for 2003. In 2002, Surrey fielded a weakened side against Northamptonshire at Whitgift due to the delayed match against Yorkshire at Headingley. David Ward was asked to play and was top-scorer with 78 in a lost match.

Birth: Guildford, Surrey 20/09/1973

Matches: 77 / 12

Batting career for Surrey:

I	NO	HS	Runs
130	11	168*	4882
105	11	97	2528
Av	100s	1000s	
41.02	11	2	
26.89	-	-	

Bowling career for Surrey:

Balls	Runs	Wkts	Av	Best	5wl
214	121	3	40.33	1-1	-
89	132	2	66.00	2-27	-

Catches: 42 21

Tests: 5, 2001-

Raised in the West Country, Ian Ward was educated at Ripley Primary School and Millfield School. There was every encouragement for cricket, his father and grandfather both having played for Devon. Something of a late developer, Ward spent a year at Surrey in 1992 before being released and spending several summers playing club and Minor Counties cricket. Averaging over 50 for the Surrey Second XI in 1996, he earned a few first-class games in 1997 and then a few more in 1998, as national call-ups created opportunities at county level.

His real breakthrough came in 1999, when he struck his maiden first-class century, 103 against Derbyshire at Derby, and in a difficult year for batsmen, he topped 1,000 runs in a season for the first time. Ward went on the England A tour that winter to New Zealand and Bangladesh, scoring 287 runs in seven matches.

His early experience of not making the grade at first-class level appears to have increased his desire to succeed with his second chance. Short in height for a professional cricketer, at 5ft 8in, he is hard-working with a solid batting technique, an excellent fielder in the covers and a good runner between the wickets. Although he failed to reach 1,000 runs in the 2000 season, Ward hit a further three centuries and played a valuable role in the Championship-winning team, forming a formidable opening partnership with Mark Butcher.

Ian Ward took part in the last England A tour to the West Indies in 2000/01, where he showed remarkable levels of concentration, batting for more than 36 hours in all to amass 769 runs including 3 hundreds and 4 fifties. At no stage did he ever dominate, but none of his teammates came close to emulating his productivity on pitches that were all low and slow, apart from Jamaica and Anguilla.

During 2001, Ian Ward played in 5 Test matches, two against Pakistan and three against Australia. Playing down the order, his highest score was 39 in his debut match at Lord's. This appeared to affect his form for Surrey, but he bounced back in 2002 to record his best year for the club. Scoring 1,708 runs for Surrey including seven centuries, four being in consecutive innings – 114 against Warwickshire at Edgbaston, 112 and 156 against Hampshire at The Rose Bowl and 118 against Leicestershire at The AMP Oval – all these three matches were won. This feat has only been accomplished three previous times by Surrey players, Tom Hayward and Jack Hobbs (twice). In the absence of Adam Hollioake and Mark Butcher, he also captained the side in several matches with great success. Away from the cricket field, Ian Ward has been seen fronting the Sky television programme on The Ashes and the World Cup with great aplomb and success.

Birth: Peckham, London 01/08/1911
Death: Cheam, Surrey 02/05/1982

Matches: 240

Batting career for Surrey:

I	NO	HS	Runs
350	68	123	6005
Av	100s	1000s	
21.29	2	-	

Bowling career for Surrey:

Balls	Runs	Wkts	Av
36907	18757	722	25.97
Best	5wl	10wM	
10-67	24	2	

Catches: 152

Eddie Watts joined Surrey as an amateur in 1933, and he immediately showed how valuable he was going to be if he could play regularly, scoring 318 runs with an average of 39.75 and taking 28 wickets at 24.85. In 1934, he joined the staff and made it clear that he had not been over-estimated by scoring 928 runs and taking 91 wickets. Against the powerful Yorkshire attack at Bradford, he made his maiden century, scoring 123 in under two hours, with 4 sixes and 14 fours. His only other first-class century came in 1936 against Hampshire at Bournemouth when he scored 116* in less than two hours.

He continued to be an essential member of the side through the years up to the Second World War. In 1937, he took 85 wickets for the county, and the following year, 1938, he headed the bowling averages with 114 wickets in Championship matches at 17.69 out of a total of 129 wickets. In 1939, he again took over 100 wickets with 106 including 10 for 67 in the second innings against Warwickshire at Edgbaston. He became only the third Surrey bowler to take ten wickets in an innings. This figure has subsequently risen to five with both

Lock and Laker having performed this rare feat.

A strongly-built man, he bowled fast medium, could swing the ball both ways and got plenty of life off the wicket – to these gifts he added a shrewd bowling brain. A fast-scoring batsman, he was a good striker of the ball, particularly through the covers, and a reliable slip. He was often the opening bowling partner of his brother-in-law, Alf Gover.

He went on two overseas tours with Sir T.E.W. Brinckman's team to South America in 1937/38 and with Sir Julien Cahn's team to New Zealand in 1938/39. In his first-class career, he scored 6,158 runs at an average of 21.41 and took 729 wickets at 26.06 apiece. He also took 155 catches. After the war, he was less effective, suffering with a knee injury, but he still took 58 Championship wickets in 1946, lying third in the averages behind Gover and Alec Bedser. He then continued to give useful assistance when required. He retired at the end of 1949 after having a very successful benefit which raised £5,000, a Surrey record at the time. He later ran a sports shop, played in the Birmingham League and coached at Whitgift School.

Birth: Elvet Hill, Co. Durham 04/10/1884
Death: Honiton, Devon 16/12/1970

Matches: 53

Batting career for Surrey:

I	NO	HS	Runs
76	8	135	1734
Av	100s	1000s	
25.50	3	-	

Bowling career for Surrey:

Balls	Runs	Wkts	Av	Best	5wl
1214	706	23	30.69	6-43	1

Catches: 25

Cyril Wilkinson was in the first team at Blundell's School before he played for Surrey between 1909 and 1920. He captained the county when they won the Championship in 1914 and again in the first two seasons following the First World War, in which he saw military service.

He had been persuaded to take over the captaincy from M.C. Bird, but then asked D.J. Knight to captain the side for some matches. *Wisden* said of him in 1914: 'He proved himself a real leader, keeping the side under firm control and managing the bowling with sound judgement.' In 1920, Percy Fender was captain from May to the end of July and, at Wilkinson's request, as things were not going very well, Wilkinson again took charge of the side for the closing matches. Again, *Wisden* said 'He proved himself in some respects the best county captain of the year. He was nearly always sound in strategy and his judgement in the management of the bowling was seldom at fault. Bringing imagination to his task, he had in his methods nothing stereotyped.'

In all first-class matches, he scored 1,173 runs, averaging 25.32, his highest innings being 135 in less than two hours against Middlesex at The Oval and, as an occasional bowler, he took 23 wickets for 31.47 runs each.

In 1914, he scored 135 against Middlesex, when Surrey totalled 502 for 5 on the first day, despite Hobbs being dismissed for four. Against the Australian Imperial Forces at The Oval in 1919, he scored 103, sharing in a stand of 146 with J.N. Crawford after Surrey had lost 5 wickets for 26. Again, he triumphed against Hampshire in 1920 at The Oval, scoring 106 in the first innings after Surrey were, at one stage, 96 for 7. In the second innings, he helped Peach in an eighth-wicket stand to see Surrey win by two wickets.

A great club cricketer, originally with Beckenham, he turned out every August for the Sidmouth team and, in 1953, at the age of sixty-nine, he hit 50 and took all ten wickets against the Nondescripts. As a hockey player, he represented England, whom he captained, and also appeared for Great Britain in the 1920 Olympic Games. He was Registrar of the Probate and Divorce Registry from 1936 to 1959.

Birth: Dartford, Kent 14/12/1853
Death: Waddon, Surrey 30/04/1919

Matches: 286

Batting career for Surrey:

I	NO	HS	Runs
378	89	83	4948
Av	100s	1000s	
17.12	-	-	

Bowling career for Surrey:

Balls	Runs	Wkts	Av	Best	5wl
37	29	0			

Catches: 522
Stumpings: 96

Tests: 4, 1888-1891/92

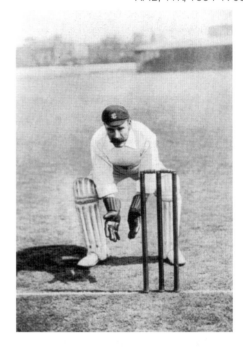

Henry Wood was the third of the four wicket-keepers who helped to sustain the fame of Surrey cricket for seventy years, following Tom Lockyer and Pooley and being in his turn succeeded by Strudwick. Of the four, Wood was the least gifted, but he did an immense amount of work and was painstaking to a great degree. The Surrey committee paid him a handsome compliment when they picked him to keep wicket for England against Australia at The Oval in 1888 and he justified their choice, being seen at his very best in the big match. Apart from that one occasion, his reputation rested almost entirely on his doings in county cricket.

Born at Dartford in Kent, he was ambitious in his young days as a cricketer to play for his native county. The Kent authorities did not realise what a good wicketkeeper he was likely to be and they let him slip out of their hands. He played in a few odd matches for Kent, but never secured a regular place in the XI. It was an engagement as ground-keeper to the Streatham club that enabled him to qualify for Surrey.

He made his first appearance for Surrey in 1884 and kept wicket for the team until 1899. He thus shared in all Surrey's triumphs under the leadership of John Shuter, and afterwards of K.J. Key. Keeping to Bowley, Beaumont,

George Lohmann and Sharpe and then to Lockwood and Tom Richardson, he had a trying time. Even on the excellent Oval wickets, his hands often suffered terribly. However, he took it all as part of the day's work and rarely complained. Apart from when his hands were very bad, he was seldom away from his post but on one occasion his absence caused disaster. He was too unwell to play against Lancashire at The Oval in 1888, when faulty wicketkeeping by his substitute undoubtedly cost Surrey the match, their only defeat in the Championship that season.

Wood was not a first-rate batsman, but he was an uncommonly good man to go in ninth or even tenth on the order. Thanks to his nerve and good hitting, he could generally be counted on for his fair share of runs. His greatest triumph as a batsman was an innings of 134* for the English team against South Africa at Cape Town in 1891/92, his second tour under W.W. Read. His first tour to that country was in 1888/89, organised by Major Warton and captained by C. Aubrey Smith. It was on this tour that his eyesight was badly affected by the glare of the sun. After he stopped playing, Wood was a county umpire from 1910 to 1912.

Birth: Jullundur, India 20/10/1947

Matches: 262 /94

Batting career for Surrey:

I	NO	HS	Runs
448	63	183*	14112
187	21	113	4899
Av	100s	1000s	
36.65	19	7	
29.51	2		

Bowling career for Surrey:

Balls	Runs	Wkts	Av	Best	5wl
1446	602	17	35.41	4-10	-
37	29	1	29.00	1-6	

Catches: 144 54

Tests: [Pakistan] 4, 1969/70-1986/87

Younis Ahmed made his first-class debut as a fourteen year old in Pakistan for the Inter Board Schools XI in March 1962. He made four Test match appearances for Pakistan, playing twice in 1969/70 against New Zealand, and then returned, 17 years and 111 days later, to play against India in 1986/87. Thickset and strong, he was a dashing left-handed batsman with a large repertoire of strokes, including a magnificent off-drive. Occasionally, he bowled either slow left-arm spin or medium pace.

Joining Surrey in 1965, he made his debut in the first team in 1967, when he played 17 Championship matches, his first century for the county being 103 against Derbyshire at The Oval. Younis had a splendid season in 1969, finishing second in the county averages and in 1970, when six players scored more than 1,000 runs. He was one of the pillars of the Surrey batting and remained a reliable force in 1971. However, in 1972, Younis was described as inconsistent, although he played some brilliant innings. He bounced back in 1973, finishing top of the Surrey averages and was sixth in the national listings. He was a great inspiration, making his highest score of 155* against Warwickshire at The Oval. In 1994, Younis was again the leading run-getter, but was less con-

sistent than the previous year, failing to score 1,000 runs for the county. He contributed greatly to Surrey's victory in the Benson & Hedges Cup.

In 1975, Younis Ahmed made his highest score of 183* against Worcestershire at Worcester, sharing a blistering seventh-wicket partnership of 173 with Intikhab Alam. Second in the county averages in 1976, his form fell away in 1977 and 1978, when he was released by the county. His contribution for Surrey in one-day matches was substantial; playing in 194 matches with a batting average of just below 30, scoring two centuries and 31 scores over 50.

He moved to Worcestershire in 1979, for which team he played 85 first-class matches and 81 one-day matches. In 1984, he went to Glamorgan, appearing in 58 first-class matches. His tours overseas included going with the Cavaliers to Jamaica in 1969/70, with the Commonwealth to Pakistan in 1970/71, with the Robins to South Africa in 1973/74 and 1974/75, with the International Wanderers to South Africa in 1974/75 and to Rhodesia in 1975/76 and with Pakistan to India in 1986/87. In his career he played 460 first-class matches, scoring 26,073 runs at an average of 40.48 with 46 centuries. He also took 49 wickets at an average of 42.87.